BUILD YOUR OWN
WALLS
& FENCES

BUILD YOUR OWN
WALLS
& FENCES

PENNY SWIFT & JANEK SZYMANOWSKI

NH
NEW HOLLAND

ACKNOWLEDGEMENTS

There are always many people to thank when a book like this one is produced. Some provide us with locations to photograph, others assist with the step-by-step projects. Professionals in various fields also offer advice and share their expertise. We cannot note them all in print, but our gratitude goes to every one.

A special thank you is extended to the people who checked the manuscript. These include experts in Australia, the United Kingdom, the United States, and South Africa, some of whom read the entire text, others just the parts that relate to their area. In particular, my thanks go to Mike Ingram, a regional director of Corobrik and Steve Crosswell, a regional director of the Portland Cement Institute, who is also an engineer. Both have assisted us on many occasions and their input is always invaluable.

Thank you, too, to Holger Rust, the inventor of Terraforce retaining blocks (now available worldwide), who not only made the step-by-step instructions on pages 51–53 possible, but who also posed for the pictures on pages 48–50 during construction of a concrete block wall on his property.

Thanks also to Andy van Niekerk, managing director of Smartstone, which manufactures reconstituted blocks. Not only is he featured building the reconstituted stone wall, but his own panel fence is included among the plans.

Harvey Downes of Centrecore made the picket fence project possible, while Neville White of Cape Gate Fence and Wire Works provided information and materials to assist with the step-by-step wire-mesh fence.

The walls and fences featured in this book were built by both professionals and by home improvement enthusiasts. Graham Viney designed the screen on page 61 for Sheila and Tom Boardman, Alan Pearson designed and built the patio screen on page 55 for his own home, and André Pugin assisted Grant and Desireé Byram with the design and construction of the charming pole fence featured on page 58.

This edition published in 2001 by
New Holland Publishers (UK) Ltd
London • Cape Town • Sydney • Auckland

24 Nutford Place, London W1H 5DQ, United Kingdom
80 McKenzie Street, Cape Town 8000, South Africa
14 Aquatic Drive, Frenchs Forest, NSW 2086, Australia
Unit 1A, 218 Lake Road, Northcote, Auckland, New Zealand

Editor Sally D. Rutherford
Designer Dean Pollard
Cover design Odette Marais and Dean Pollard
Design manager Petal Palmer
Design assistant Lellyn Creamer
Illustrator Clarence Clarke
DTP conversion Jacques le Roux

Reproduction in Cape Town by cmyk prepress
Printed and bound in Slovakia by Slovenska Grafia

ISBN 1 85974 748 5

10 9 8 7 6 5

Also available in Afrikaans as:
Bou Jou Eie Mure en Heinings

CONTENTS

Garden walls and fences are invaluable elements within all garden schemes. They provide security, add privacy, and are frequently used to define the boundary of a property. They may also be erected specifically to block out unsightly views or service areas, to furnish some protection from the elements, or to provide a perfect backdrop or support for plants. Whatever the size or style of your garden, these varied structures also give you the opportunity to subdivide and re-organise the shape and function of your outdoor space.

The concept of enclosing areas around homes and dividing parts of the garden to create separate, often private, areas is nothing new. Ancient civilisations used walls and hedges to create secluded courtyards and kitchen gardens. The most famous wall is probably the Great Wall of China, built in about 200 BC, a monumental 2.414 km masonry structure which still stands today. In medieval times, enclosures were largely constructed as a means of defence, and walled paradise gardens (or parks) were popular. Early European gardens often included walls and neatly clipped hedges to introduce a feeling of formality, while the cottage gardens of 18th-century Britain featured rustic fences, stone walls and hedgerows planted with a mix of shrubs and trees. Many of the most famous late-Victorian gardeners used walls, fences, screens and hedges to create secret gardens and a series of 'rooms' outdoors. The materials chosen for these structures have varied over time depending on availability and cost, as well as the purpose of the barrier. Whilst the earliest walls were made of stone, bricks have been used for many centuries: as long ago as the Middle Ages walls were built from irregular, handmade bricks. Rustic timber fencing and hedges have been used for thousands of years.

Nowadays expense is a primary consideration, but the design, size and style of your garden, as well as the type of barrier you prefer, are all vital factors. Furthermore, the architecture of your house should also be considered, especially if you are planning a solid structure.

The method of construction is another very important consideration. If you plan to build or erect your own wall or fence, it is important to have (or to learn) the necessary skills. Some materials are more difficult to work with than others, but most structures can be tackled successfully by the competent handyman. Alternatively, if you feel you cannot lay your own bricks or erect the fencing of your choice, or do not have the time to do so, you can always employ someone to do the work for you. And whether you plan to do-it-yourself or to use the services of professionals, this book will be an invaluable guide, offering good ideas and advice from the design and planning stages right through to the construction phase.

The first part of the book will help you choose the best type of wall or fencing for your particular needs. It illustrates a range of effective finishes and recommends a wide variety of suitable materials for every building method. There are also many imaginative suggestions for combining materials and incorporating distinctive features to tranform an ordinary design into something special.

A timber panel fence forms a perfect backdrop for pretty plants.

A simple, precast picket fence.

Post-and-rail fences are popular.

Elaborate cast-ironwork may be set between plain, rendered brick pillars for a period look.

Critical cost implications are considered in general terms and the most common building codes, regulations and restrictions which affect DIY builders are discussed in the relevant sections.

With the information supplied, you will be in a position to site the structure most effectively within the constraints of boundaries and any servitudes, liens or other legal restrictions.

Since most walls and fences incorporate gates or doors, this aspect is considered in some detail, as is the importance of including these elements in the landscaping plan as a whole. Security, which can be a vital factor, is dealt with separately, with an emphasis on maintaining an attractive façade. Retaining walls as well as some less substantial screens are discussed, along with hedges and other planted barriers and borders.

A comprehensive range of accepted construction methods is explained,

from blockwork and bricklaying to basic carpentry and simple metalwork. The necessary tools are clearly itemised, and a table is given on page 36 to help you to estimate the quantities of materials needed.

To simplify construction for beginners, photographic step-by-step instructions are featured in some detail. These illustrate how to lay both a facebrick and a stone block wall with supporting pillars; a simple method of building a substantial boundary wall with hollow concrete blocks, and how to render it; how to erect an attractive timber picket fence and hang a homemade gate; as well as how to make an open lattice screen from timber laths. Also shown are proven techniques commonly used to install a wire-mesh fence, so that it is properly tensioned and braced, and the procedure for the construction of a 1.2 m-high retaining wall from interlocking concrete terrace blocks.

In the latter half of the book, a total of 10 project plans are provided, together with a detailed list of materials required for each, and a simple list of guidelines to help you tackle it systematically.

Since dimensions, boundary lines and other factors will be sure to vary, most of the plans relate to a section of the structure; for instance, one panel of a fence, or the length of wall between two pillars. The designs are suitable for most gardens, but formal building plans will be necessary in many areas. You are advised to check with your local authority before putting any of the plans into action.

The designs chosen incorporate a variety of materials and range from a simple yet attractive trellis screen suitable for use alongside a patio, to a solid boundary wall with generous planters. A picket gate is included in one of the plans, and pillars in several. All may be adapted to meet your particular needs.

Walls and fences are used to enclose properties and frequently to divide gardens into several distinct areas. Most are permanent in nature, although some less substantial screens and enclosures may be moved and resited with reasonably little effort. The motivations for building a wall or erecting a fence or screen vary but, whatever your needs, the value of thorough planning and careful preparation must never be underestimated. Every property and each individual garden plan is different, so it is vital to ensure that any structure, however simple, blends with the general scheme and that it complements your home. It is essential to consider the full range of available materials at an early stage, and to cost the project before work begins.

FUNCTION

Even though the two most obvious functions of any type of wall or fence are enclosure and division, every structure you build will have a more specific role to play.

Those constructed around your property may screen the garden from passing traffic, effectively reducing the noise of the traffic and at the same time creating a welcome feeling of privacy. They also may provide a practical shield from prevailing winds, and may filter the sun. On the other hand, walls and fences may simply define your boundaries, or act as a support for climbers and creepers, or security may be their primary function.

Walls or fences built within the garden itself have even more functions. Walls may be built to establish courtyards or secluded areas within the garden. A low wall may be purely decorative, visually dividing one section of the garden from another, or it may be functional, perhaps incorporating a planter, water feature or a simple seating design. Even small and apparently insignificant structures

may play an important role in the landscape plan, defining flower beds or perhaps demarcating a patio.

If you live in a rural area and have livestock (horses, cows or sheep, for instance), or even if you have dogs, suitable fencing will contain the animals and prevent them from roaming. If you have a swimming pool, pool fencing and self-closing gates are essential to protect toddlers and children from possible harm.

Retaining walls have a practical function, and are a frequent component of sloping gardens. They must be designed and built with care to ensure that they are strong enough to support the earth they will retain, and will not collapse unexpectedly (see page 23).

SITE

While the function of a fence or wall will to some extent determine its site, you will find there are usually many location options and a host of other factors which must be examined.

One of the most important considerations will be any legal restrictions which affect the location of walls and fences. The most obvious is the demarcated boundary line of any property. However, there may be other factors which prevent you from building a wall or fencing an area at a particular spot. There may also be a legal requirement compelling you to erect some form of barrier, for instance around a swimming pool.

The first step is to check your own boundaries. If necessary have them

This picket fence around the boundary is painted white to match an internal lattice screen.

professionally surveyed to avoid any future disputes with neighbours. If you intend building on the actual boundary line, you will share ownership of the structure, even if your neighbour does not contribute towards the cost of it. The ideal situation is to get the cooperation of your neighbour, to mutually agree on the design and to share the costs. If this is not possible and the situation is unacceptable, a possible solution would be to site the wall or fence at least 150 mm in from your side of the boundary.

The next step is to check any other restrictions. Most of these are imposed by local authorities and relate to all residential land in an area, even though it is sometimes possible to obtain a variance or waiver to disregard them. In some case there may be a servitude, lien or other legal restraint which relates to your property in particular. For instance, a registered servitude or lien could allow other people access to an established footpath on your property. This would, in effect, prevent you from fencing it off unless a gate was provided.

Having determined the limitations, you can explore all the remaining possibilities in relation to your needs. If, for instance, you are building a wall for privacy, the front boundary line may seem at first to be the most obvious place to site it. Many people, however, prefer to leave the front garden open to the road, and to enclose a more secluded area for relaxation and entertainment. This is usually the cheaper option and a viable one, unless the need for security is the main priority. Similarly, a pool fence may be sited two or three metres from the perimeter of a swimming pool, or you may include more of the garden in this area and use an existing garden wall as one side of the enclosure.

DRAWING PLANS
Unless you already have a site plan, drawing one will make the planning much easier. Draw it to scale using ordinary graph paper, indicating where all buildings and existing structures are located. You will need to know the

A semi-detached house relies on a timber structure to screen the front garden for privacy.

Although a low wall defines this boundary, it does not shield the roses from view.

A low facebrick wall combines beautifully with shrubs and trees along a boundary.

The curved design of an unusual brick-and-stone wall adds character to the entrance.

dimensions of the site itself and of buildings, and distances between the various structures and boundaries. Mark these and the direction of true north. Draw in any landscaping features (trees, pathways, large rocks and so on). Existing walls, fences and hedges should also be shown, along with established shrubs and flower beds, and good view sites which you do not want to obstruct. Then mark in and label any sections of the garden which have a specific function, such as a patio, vegetable or herb garden, utility area with washing line and so on. If possible, spend some time in the garden noting sun patterns and prevailing winds, and indicate these on the scale plan too.

If it is done accurately, this plan will give a very good picture of the site and will help you to decide exactly where the garden should be enclosed or divided. Do not draw the position of any proposed walls, fencing or screens directly onto your plan. Instead, mark them on tracing paper and make several overlays of the various options that appeal to you.

A sloping property is a little more difficult to deal with, particularly if walls or fencing are to traverse steep or undulating ground. If you have a contour map of the site, refer to this; otherwise you may be able to simply label areas which could pose problems. If you do have a slope, you must decide whether you wish to step your wall or fence, or whether you need to build a retaining wall.

Neither walls nor fences have to be straight, and this is something you should remember when siting the structure. Furthermore, you do not have to remove all obstacles: a tree or attractive rock could be incorporated very effectively into the plan, often creating a unique feature.

Once you have decided where you are going to build your walls or fences, you should do more accurate drawings indicating the dimensions of posts, pillars, rails and so on. This will not only help you to visualise the design, but will enable you to accurately cost the project (see page 12).

HEIGHT AND DIMENSIONS

There are certain practical points to consider when determining wall or fence height, ranging from personal needs to the requirements of any local authority, and the necessity to use sound building principles.

If, for instance, you want to build a wall that will give you privacy from neighbours and passing traffic, it will have to be reasonably high with adequate foundations, expansion joints and supporting pillars or piers. You may also need to build in brick reinforcement. If you want to build something that will shield an entertainment patio from the wind, it is often better to opt for a structure that will allow the wind to pass through it. A perforated screen wall or slatted fence is often the best solution here, although it is important to ensure that it will withstand buffeting from strong winds. Solid walls sometimes precipitate turbulence, which can be very unpleasant and may cause damage to plants and patio furniture.

The height of any wall or fence is usually covered in local codes and planning or building regulations, although requirements and restrictions vary. Check how high you can build without plans and whether there will be any special steps your local council will insist you take when building it.

Even if there are no official constraints, common sense will tell you to adhere to fundamental building principles, and to seek advice if you are not sure what height and dimensions are acceptable. Local conditions, including wind and snow, are a vital consideration.

A low wall – around a flower bed, for example – can be built as a single thickness of stretcher-bond brickwork, but high boundary walls must not only be thicker, they should also incorporate reinforcing piers at regular intervals.

If you do not have any guidelines, you can safely build a half-brick garden wall about 100 mm thick to a height of 450 mm without piers, and to about 700 mm if two-brick piers are provided at 3 m centres. A thicker

The strong lines of a metal fence add interest and provide security rather than privacy.

Flower boxes follow the stepped lines of a solid brick wall which has been rendered.

Precast concrete panels, moulded to look like facebrick, were chosen for their texture.

COST

There is rarely a time when cost is not a major consideration in a building programme. It is sometimes possible to stagger the building, doing essential projects first (for example, security fencing or boundary walling), and then building additional features like screen walls and other dividing structures within the garden at a later stage, when additional funds are available. Or you can divide each project itself into several stages.

Budget constraints may mean that you are forced to opt for one of the cheaper wall or fencing types, particularly if you cannot complete the project in stages. If you do have to compromise, make sure that whatever you build still meets your needs and fulfils the function for which it was intended (see page 8). You will not be saving money if you have to replace what you have built in a few years' time, simply because it does not provide adequate privacy or is not an effective barrier to strong winds. A brick wall will certainly be more expensive than a picket fence, but if security is your principal motive for building a barrier, you cannot even consider this type of fencing. On the other hand, a relatively inexpensive 1.8 m-high wire-mesh fence may be an acceptable alternative, even though it will not create privacy without the addition of a plant screen.

A sensible approach is to cost the project thoroughly in the planning stage. To do this properly, you will have to establish exactly what quantity of materials is required (see page 36). Everything should be included, from cement, sand and aggregate or crushed stone for foundations and footings, to all the nails, screws and other hardware you are likely to need. If you are building a wall that is to be rendered, do not forget to include paint, and if you are working with timber, allow a sum for any necessary wood coatings or preservatives. If you are planning to use the services of professionals or to employ labour to assist you, be sure to include these amounts in your total costing.

one-brick wall may be built to a height of at least 1.35 m (or 18 courses) without piers, and to 1.8 m with 440 mm square piers at 3 m centres.

Half-brick walls should never be built to retain soil. Retaining walls should be at least 200 mm thick and must always incorporate weep holes for drainage, to prevent excessive accumulation of water behind the structure. Limitations on height, wall thickness and pier size are generally stringent, as severe damage may result from the collapse of even the lowest retaining wall.

Certain fence types and styles are better suited to different heights. A picket or post-and-rail fence can form an attractive boundary line, but these designs are both low. A panel fence, on the other hand, may be built substantially higher, as long as you provide adequate support for the material used.

MATERIALS

Having decided what to build, you will have to choose suitable materials for construction. The factors already discussed will all influence your choice, but you should also be guided by a thorough knowledge of all the available options (see pages 20–29).

While some materials will blend with any style of house, continuity is an important factor which should not be overlooked. Aim for harmony, and select materials which complement one another. For instance, if yours is a facebrick house, the same brick will be an obvious choice for the garden wall. If you want fencing, consider a neat palisade fence, which will suit the more formal finish of facebrick, but add a touch of rusticity. For a cottage-style home with walls smothered in pretty creepers and climbers, a hedge, stone wall or picket fence will be more complementary and appropriate.

In certain instances, there may be a variety of suitable and appropriate materials. For instance, a wall that is to be rendered can be built with clay bricks or concrete blocks, and screen walls with any number of perforated block designs. Similarly, a panel fence can be constructed with wooden slats, exterior-grade plywood, tempered hardboard (masonite) or even water-resistant particle board (chipboard). If you opt for wire fencing, there will be a range of options for both the support posts and the wire mesh or netting. Consider both appearance and cost before making a decision.

There are numerous professionals who can assist by offering valuable advice, designing structures and drawing up plans, undertaking the actual construction or by organising and overseeing the entire project for you. You will need to decide how much of the work you want to do yourself, and then identify the areas where help is needed.

Design

If yours is to be a purely functional fence or wall, without any special features, you probably will not require any assistance to design it. However, input from a professional can make all the difference, not only to the appearance of the finished product, but also in the choice of location and type of structure you build. It will also be helpful if the structure is a substantial one which requires special skills.

If you are involving a landscape architect or designer in the garden scheme, it makes sense to ask the same person to design your walls and fences. Similarly, if you have used the services of an architect to design the house or any additional building work, you can ensure a continuity of style if you hire the same professional now.

Specialist companies sometimes have their own designers, although many concentrate on structural rather than aesthetic elements.

Plans

If plans are required, these will identify the position of walls or fences and specify their height on a site plan. You may need to indicate the contours of the land and, depending on the type of construction used, include various sections and elevations. Whilst there is unlikely to be anything to stop you from drawing these up yourself, official rules and regulations are usually quite specific in their requirements. Unless you are familiar with these, it is therefore often wise to ask for professional assistance.

Since an architect often includes these elements in a house plan, and a landscaper incorporates them in his or her garden layout, either of these professionals may be approached. Most will work on an hourly basis as a consultant, or get as involved as you want them to be, even ordering materials and overseeing construction if necessary.

If you know exactly what you want, a draughtsman will draw up the plans on your behalf. This is a particularly good option if you are going to do the building yourself, or even hire sub-contractors, as their fees are generally much lower than the other professionals.

Building contractors and specialist fencing companies will usually include the submission of plans in their service, but they do not always have design skills.

Building

Apart from major retaining structures which frequently require the services of an engineer, most brick, block or stone walls can be built by competent DIYers. Fences, too, may be erected by handymen without any special skills. But there are basic building methods and techniques which must be adhered to if you hope to achieve a professional finish (see pages 30–35). It is imperative that you do not hire untrained or inexperienced labourers (however enthusiastic) to do the building work for you. If you do not have the confidence to tackle the project yourself, a fencing or building contractor may be the answer. However, this will cost more and so you must be sure you are paying for quality work. Ask for references and look at other structures built by this person.

Another option is to employ independent artisans. Bricklayers, plasterers, pavers and carpenters will work at an hourly rate or set a fee for the job. You will need to order the materials and supervise your labour force, so it pays to familiarise yourself with basic building principles. These people are not usually difficult to locate, although you will need to obtain reliable references. Ideally, employ artisans who are known to you or to associates; or check the classified advertisements in your local newspaper.

An ambitious rendered wall designed by a professional.

Concrete facebrick and metalwork installed by a specialist.

The importance of the design and style of walls and fences should not be underestimated. These are permanent, often costly, structures which form the framework of any garden. Once in place, they are not easily removed, so it is important that whatever you decide to construct, erect or, in the case of hedging, plant, suits your house and your garden.

Unfortunately, the visual impact of enclosures and dividing barriers is often overlooked, with the result that many of them do nothing much to enhance the look of a garden. Yet, with a little extra thought, effort and imagination, even the simplest, most inexpensive type of barrier can be improved by imaginative design.

Whilst there is no doubt that most boundary walls and fences have a primarily practical function, the very fact that they surround the property means they provide visitors with their first impression of your home.

Boundary structures are highly visible, so attention should be given to both the exterior façade and the appearance of the inside surfaces. The positioning of gates and doors is also very important.

Materials do not have to match those used elsewhere, but they should always complement the finish of the house. Furthermore, the design and style should be consistent with existing architectural elements and with any theme which is apparent in the garden.

Enclosures and screens located within the garden have a variety of functions (see page 29), and some will be more conspicuous than others. The trick is to aim for a pleasing visual effect and continuity. Remember that whatever you construct must form a natural part of the landscaping plan as a whole.

DESIGN BASICS

There are no rigid rules when it comes to garden design, but the importance of a good basic plan cannot be overemphasized. As trees and shrubs take years to develop, it is important to create a sound framework so that they are integrated in the best possible way into any structures you build.

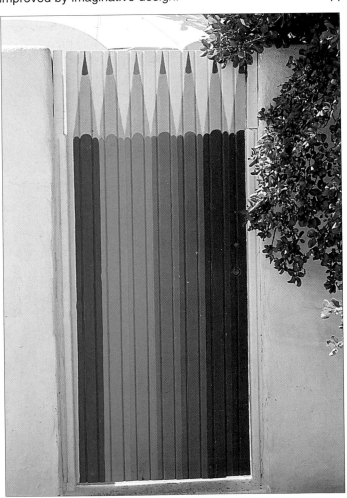

Colourful pencil crayons are an enticement to what lies beyond.

A bamboo palisade fence sets the style for an unusual garden.

Latticework set between brick pillars screens a parking area.

Whether you are starting from scratch or adding to or even simply enclosing an old garden, successful design demands a clear plan of action. On pages 9–10, the importance of an accurate site plan is discussed. In addition to this, you will need to establish whether the layout you are planning is to be essentially formal or informal, and then decide if you are going to follow a theme or establish a particular style.

Garden designers talk about two types of landscaping – hard and soft. The first, which includes the erection of fences and construction of walls, relates to all the hard, rigid materials which may be used to create a basic, static shell. Soft landscaping, on the other hand, refers to trees, foliage, flowers, hedges and so on; in other words, the natural elements which provide a vital softening effect.

Since structural work is, by its very nature, messy and often disruptive, you will need to complete as much hard landscaping as possible before starting to plant.

Layout

The layout of any garden will be determined by numerous factors, ranging from the size and shape of the plot to personal preference. It will also be affected by the style, if any, you choose to follow.

It is important to decide whether this arrangement will, in general, be formal or informal. Not only will this help you select the shape and form of flower beds and the type of plants to be included, but also the manner in which the property should be enclosed and, if necessary, divided.

Formal gardens are characterised by symmetry and a carefully planned balance of all the elements involved. All except the most rustic types of material may be used.

There is usually little you can do to correct or alter the position of a boundary wall unless you choose to move it in from the actual perimeter of the property. Facebrick or neatly rendered walls may be used to good effect around the perimeter, while

A modern metal fence is both functional and attractive.

clipped hedges and neat latticework fences are perfect for internal screens. If planters and other features are to be incorporated in a wall, ensure that these fit the formal look.

Informal gardens are typified by irregular-shaped flower beds and gentle curves. However, even though straight lines should generally be avoided in garden design, this principle need not apply to the walls and fences which are built or erected within this area. A simple brick wall will provide a good backdrop to any scheme, while a straightforward post-and-panel fence will provide a good, solid surface for supporting climbing plants.

An informal garden is a good place to use really rustic materials, including random stone and waney board. Wire mesh is not particularly attractive on its own, but if covered with plants or shielded by a screen of foliage, it will complement the informal appearance of your garden.

Style

There are a several readily identifiable garden styles, ranging from the typical cottage garden to classical designs which imitate those laid out by various French and Italian landscapers during the Renaissance.

If your house is built in a specific architectural style, you may wish to continue the theme to the garden.

If so, both hard and soft landscaping should be in keeping with the genre. For instance, it would be a pity to build a high wall around a quaint thatched cabin if you plan to plant a traditional cottage garden. Here, a picket fence or low hedge will be a more appropriate choice, as passers-by will be able to see the haphazard abundance of colour which typifies this style. Whitewashed walls which shelter private patios and enclose intimate courtyards are a feature of Mediterranean-style homes, while bamboo screens and latticework will fit a Japanese theme. Post-and-rail fencing will lend a rural feel, and decorative wrought iron can help introduce a touch of Victorian style.

If you are not certain which approach to take, the best advice is to keep walls and fences functional and simple. That way they are more likely to blend with your scheme and to keep your garden stylish.

Theme

In addition to style, which is in itself a theme of sorts, there are many other themes which can be either carried throughout the garden or confined to individual areas.

The best places to get ideas for garden themes are local public gardens and parks, and, of course, gardening books and magazines.

There is little doubt that one of the most popular themes is colour. One can use either a single hue or a combination of several. The question is whether to limit the theme to flowering shrubs and blooms, or to extend it to accessories and man-made structures. It is a personal choice, but garden walls and fences are rarely designed to match a colour scheme. It is usually better to allow these structures to act as a natural foil to the plants and other features which display the chosen shades.

Where several themes are introduced within a garden, a variety of partitions and borders may be considered. A screen wall may be the choice alongside an entertainment patio, while a pretty picket fence may be considered a more appropriate means of separating and shielding the kitchen garden. A latticework structure or wrought-iron fence might be the preferred option around a rose garden, particularly if it is to be smothered with rambling roses or climbers.

Where the theme is herbs and the layout is formal, it makes sense to introduce a clipped hedge of lavender, box or myrtle. If you do not have the patience to plant and tend to these, a low wall is an option. Or consider a plain fence, perhaps to be used as a frame for some climbing plants.

FINISH AND EFFECT

Walls and fences may be as plain or ornate as you wish. This will depend partly on the style, if any, you have chosen to emulate, as well as the materials you decide to use. For instance, planters may be incorporated into the design of just about any brick or concrete block wall design, but they will not be feasible if precast panels are to be used. Similarly, the finish chosen for the top of a picket fence may be quite elaborate, whilst the posts of most other types of fencing are usually kept simple.

If you want to introduce colour by painting the structure, it stands to reason that a suitable material must be used for its construction; avoid facebricks, rustic timber that has not been debarked, uneven waney board and stone.

Capping

Laid along the top of brick or stone walls to aid drainage, capping is often the most decorative feature of these otherwise plain structures, and attention should be paid to its detail. Materials used are often the same as those employed for the wall itself, although this is not always the case. For instance, facebricks may be laid to finish a wall that has been rendered (plastered) and painted, or quarry tiles

may be set atop a plain brick wall. Since capping which is slightly wider than the wall will effectively direct water away from the vertical surface, sloping roof tiles or shaped precast concrete capping set on a neatly rendered structure are particularly suitable materials and usually very attractive options.

Where matching capping bricks are available, these may be preferred, or you can fashion a shaped top with bricks and mortar. For solid facebrick walls, it is quite effective to use bricks laid on-edge. Similarly, pieces of split stone may be set on-edge atop a natural or dressed stone wall to finish it off. When building pierced or open screen walls, a continuous capping of stretcher bond will produce a nice, clean finish.

In previous centuries, walls were sometimes designed with a much wider, rooflike capping than we would use today. Although modern materials generally negate the need for a bulky protective capping, this finishing touch can add authenticity to certain styles. For instance, formal Oriental cappings were traditionally ornate, with flat or half-round tiles laid to create a narrow peaked cap along the entire length of the wall, and the Victorians sometimes created a pitch along the tops of walls and used tiles for capping.

A splash of colour adds interest to this gate.

Reconstituted stone blocks are used to create a visual theme.

This traditional hurdle archway combines well with a simple picket fence.

A modern and unusual gateway.

The entrance to a garden will always give the first impression of what lies beyond. The entrance may also set the style of the property, including the house itself. A door within the garden adds interest and tempts one to enter, even if its very purpose is to prevent one from doing so; and most gates will allow a glimpse, at the very least, of what is on the other side.

Most properties have at least one gate or external door which is located either on the boundary or, less frequently, within the garden itself. These are planned in numerous styles and constructed from a wide variety of materials. Although each has the obvious function of allowing people to pass through the wall or fence of which it is a part, its specific purpose should be carefully considered.

Do you want to encourage people to enter the door or gate, or would you prefer a design which obstructs access? Is this an entry point for vehicles? If so, will pedestrians also use it? Even if security is not a major factor, do you need a secure gate to keep children and animals inside?

While the fence or wall will be the initial guide to the type of gate or door you provide, you will need to decide how secure or substantial the arrangement you provide must be to meet your needs.

Many gardens have more than one entrance, and not all of these are through a gate or door. Even if the area is fenced, an arch or simple gap in a hedge or fence may be sufficient for your needs. This is also the case within the garden, where a variety of gaps and arches allow one to wander from one section to another without the hindrance of opening and shutting anything at all.

Obviously, where security is an important factor and you do not want people to have free access to (or through) the garden, you will be sure to need a well-designed door or gate which prevents this from happening. While a modest wooden gate or typically Victorian wrought-iron one may be quite adequate and perfectly in keeping with the style of your home and garden, if the gate is there to prevent people from entering, or peeping into, the garden you will need a more substantial design, with handles or locks which cannot be easily released from the outside.

The size of the gate will usually be determined by function. For instance, where there is a path, and a gate or door is provided for the exclusive use of pedestrians, the entrance will usually be in proportion to the width of this walkway. The height of any gate or door which is fitted will also match these proportions. Often gateways within the garden are narrow and low, although a more lofty and solid wooden door is undoubtedly a better option in a screen wall planned to hide an area from view. If the gate is to admit vehicles, it will need to be wide enough to do this comfortably. For security reasons you may want to consider those which are remote-controlled (see page 19).

Although there is something to be said for unusual portals which demand attention and make an architectural statement, this approach should be avoided by those with no design experience at all. Rather keep gates and fences simple. A safe rule of thumb is to ensure that the design complements the style of the house, perhaps duplicating features like arches and columns, or simply by framing the house in a sympathetic way.

Materials chosen should generally be consistent or analogous with those used for fences and walls. Timber and metal are probably the two most popular types of material and both may be combined successfully with most enclosures, from planted hedges to solid brick or block walls. Wooden gates usually create a more modest impression, while wrought iron can be as simple or elaborate as you wish.

Capping above an entrance adds character and style.   *A modern wall and driveway gate painted white to fit the theme.*

Pillars and piers

Often incorporated in walls for structural reasons, pillars and piers can be quite decorative features in themselves. Topped with orbs and spheres, finials, urns and other ornaments, they will add character and charm to any garden style. This is particularly useful when pillars are used as part of a design which incorporates metal- or latticework. You may even choose to decorate them with pots or ornate containers, using plants to create another dimension.

Of course, it is not necessary to embellish every pillar in the structure – many people prefer to limit the use of these embellishments to gateways and entrances (see page 17).

Niches, alcoves and arches

Primarily decorative features, niches, alcoves and arches are common in many period gardens. Even though some of the oldest walled gardens featured recesses which were used for storage, nowadays niches and alcoves are more commonly used to display statuary and sculpture, or simply to add interest. Plaques, wall-mounted sundials and even wall pots may all be mounted within these recesses. Whilst most traditional niches are probably oval or arched in shape, there is no reason why they should not be squared off.

Arches are commonly constructed to support gates and doorways in walls.

However, this is not always the case, and they may be included in the structure to frame a niche, plaque or even a water feature, in which case there will obviously be no access through the archway.

Some Mediterranean-style walls include arches as a design feature, either as points of entry or as openings above ground level in which to place potted plants. Where security is a factor, these arches may be secured with wrought-ironwork.

Planters

A favourite design feature for walls built with bricks, blocks or stone, planters give you the opportunity to soften the hard lines of any structure. They are specially suitable for the exterior of boundary walls and for smaller patios and courtyards where plants will be well contained and generally easier to tend than any established in adjacent beds.

The possible configurations are endless: a parallel low wall built alongside the main structure will create a continuous planter, while recessed compartments will create a more punctuated effect. In situations where a wall cuts across the corner of a property diagonally (some countries have legislation which limits the construction of walls at traffic intersections because of loss of visibility) it is sometimes possible to use the 'lost' piece of land by building

a low planter into the corner. On a patio, planters may be used to create a decorative and interesting stepped effect in the wall.

Paint

Undoubtedly a magical decorating tool for use both inside and outside the house, paint gives instant colour and verve to an exterior. Both walls and fences may be painted (presuming the material is suitable, see page 16) in a single hue or combination of shades, while the location of some structures offers the opportunity of an even more adventurous approach in the form of murals or trompe-l'oeil.

The decision to introduce colour will be an intensely personal one, which should be in keeping with the scheme employed for the house itself. Usually, the most appropriate approach is to match or harmonise the paint finish used on garden walls with the exterior of the house. However, wooden fences may, quite successfully, pick up contrasting accent hues. For instance, a bold blue picket fence might look quite odd around some houses, but if the style is right and the window frames and doors are painted in the same colour, it could look remarkable.

White paint is frequently and very successfully used for all kinds of enclosures and screens. This colour is particularly suitable for formal fencing, latticework screens and all kinds of rendered (plastered) walls.

Spikes set along the top of a garden wall will deter intruders.

An attactive yet reasonably solid automatic gate is a good option for larger properties.

The earliest walls and enclosures were erected for security or safety. In medieval times, solid walls were built for defence, to create an impregnable barrier to thwart the enemy. Early fences were constructed to protect crops from foraging animals or to stop wild animals from attacking stock.

Generally, walls are more secure than fences, but a substantial board fence or a sturdy metal one will also provide a barrier which will deter would-be intruders. Height is important though, as a low enclosure which can be scaled easily will not create an effective obstacle.

Many people believe that a solid enclosure is preferable for security, since potential intruders cannot see into the property – perhaps these walls are effective psychological deterrents.

However, once on the inside of a solid structure, burglars will be out of view of passers-by, and may well take advantage of the added privacy afforded by the solid wall or fence. It is necessary, therefore, to take additional steps such as effective lighting, an alarm system and perhaps burglar bars on the windows to protect your house and belongings.

Remember, too, that any boundary barrier is only as strong as its weakest link, and this is usually the entrance. Doors and gates (see page 17) should be high enough to prevent people from climbing over them, and they must be secure. Generally, it is a good idea to make them the same height as the perimeter enclosure. Furthermore, they should be kept closed and locked at all times: if they are not, anybody can walk in.

Remote control is a great advantage when it comes to opening and shutting entrances. Not only will this enable you to enter your property and close the gate again without leaving your car, but you can also open pedestrian access points this way. A two-way communication system will enable you to speak to visitors without having to open the door or gate; a viewer will allow you to see that person.

Some of the less attractive approaches to security involve the use of barbed wire, spikes and other hazardous materials. Not only do these look ugly, but they can be dangerous and have frequently resulted in legal action against the property owner. Furthermore, in some parts of the world use of these materials is restricted. Check with your local authority before installing something that is intended to cut, impale or give an electric shock to intruders.

Handsome wooden panels set neatly between sturdy pillars on a boundary.

Precast concrete units are bolted together to form a solid fence structure.

Walls and fences come in many different types, from random stone and brick structures to timber palings, picket panels and wire-mesh fences. The classification of barriers and enclosures of all kinds is determined to a large extent by the materials which are used; however, the various categories also depend on the method of construction employed.

The decision about which type to use will depend on numerous factors. By now you will know where your fence or wall is to be sited and you will probably have some idea of the design you want. Before you make a final choice, consider all the options carefully. Apart from aesthetic considerations, evaluate all the practical aspects of the different types. Determine the cost of the materials required, ascertain how durable they will be, and establish the probable maintenance the finished structure will need. It is generally accepted that solid brick or stone walls are more durable than other types, but they are also more costly and take longer to construct than a simple wire enclosure or post-and-rail or picket fence. On the other hand, if timber fencing is to last indefinitely, the wood must be well maintained and repaired immediately there is any deterioration.

If you are going to erect the fence or build the wall yourself, make certain you have all the necessary skills before you start (see pages 30–35). If you are in any doubt about your capabilities, employ a professional to help you or opt for a different type of structure altogether.

WALLS

Although walls may be built in a vast range of styles, there are only a few different types, and these are generally categorised by the materials used for construction. Most walls are built with bricks or blocks made either from clay or concrete. Certain types of wall are best rendered (plastered), whilst others are intended to be left as they are. Other possible materials include natural stone, where this is available, and various types of timber.

Blocks

Versatile and generally cost-effective, blocks are frequently used to build garden walls. Even though some are large and bulky, most are hollow and reasonably easy to handle.

There are various types of blocks available in a wide range of sizes and finishes. Most are laid in the same way as ordinary bricks (see pages 34–35), and are equally suitable for the construction of decorative features, including flower boxes and archways. Various concrete modular blocks are useful for constructing retaining walls.

The most usual type of block is made from concrete, although adobe (mud) blocks can be found in the United States and clay blocks (maxi bricks) are manufactured in some parts of the world. Glass blocks are also available, although these are more commonly used inside the house.

Standard building blocks are generally quicker to lay than ordinary bricks, and the plain kinds are much cheaper per square metre.

Plain concrete blocks, which are normally hollow and relatively lightweight, will enable you to build a good, sturdy wall; however, they are not particularly attractive and may be faced with a decorative skin (which will obviously increase your costs) or rendered and then painted.

Screen blocks have pierced patterns which add a decorative touch and make them ideal for walls intended to form a partial partition. They can also be used quite effectively to create feature areas within solid structures.

To produce an attractive, regular pattern, these blocks are laid in a stack bond, with no overlaps. For this reason it is essential to construct supporting piers or pillars at regular intervals, which will give added strength and stability, and to include some horizontal wire reinforcement (brickforce) between courses.

Reconstituted (reconstructed) stone blocks are made from concrete which is coloured and moulded to create a textured 'stone' face. Available in numerous sizes (including jumper blocks which span two or more courses), they enable you to create walls which look as though they have been built with natural dressed stone.

Concrete modular blocks intended for the construction of retaining walls are available in a variety of designs. Some systems are interlinked, while others interlock on the horizontal and/or vertical plane. Most of these hollow units can be planted once the wall has been erected. Some are suitable only for light terrace walls rather than for more substantial gravity-retaining walls, which depend on their own mass for stability.

When using modular concrete blocks for a retaining wall, it is essential to follow the manufacturer's instructions. It may also be necessary to consult an engineer for more detailed specifications in terms of your site.

Adobe blocks are common in parts of the United States, particularly the south-west, where they have been made for centuries from the local mud. Nowadays these environmentally friendly blocks are stabilised with asphalt to make them stronger and impervious to water, and consequently are longer lasting. Inexpensive in the areas where they are made, adobe blocks are relatively heavy and cumbersome to work with. They are not available in other countries.

Clay blocks (sometimes referred to as maxi bricks) are manufactured in exactly the same way as ordinary clay bricks, but they are larger in size and can be laid more quickly, and with less mortar. Like non-face bricks, they are intended to be rendered.

Concrete blocks were used to build this pleasing wall.

An attractive screen wall built from concrete facebricks.

Clay facebricks are a popular choice for garden boundary walls.

Glass blocks are manufactured so that they may be laid with mortar in the normal way. They are hollow and come in a variety of sizes and finishes. Even though they are more commonly used for walls within the house itself, they may be successfully incorporated in garden screen walls where some visibility is required.

Bricks

A readily available, universally acceptable material, brick is a popular choice for the garden. It is long lasting, versatile and blends well with virtually all architectural styles. Since bricks are relatively small in size and therefore easy to handle, it is also reasonably simple for most people to lay bricks single-handed, which increases their appeal for DIY builders.

Although the dimensions of different types of brick may vary slightly, their universally regular shape makes them easy to bond in neat patterns (a task which is considerably more difficult when building with a material like natural stone). A further advantage is that they may be laid effortlessly in both straight and curved lines, and can be used to develop a multitude of decorative features, including planters, niches and arches.

Manufactured in a wide range of colours and textures, both facebricks and common or non-face bricks, which are intended for rendering, are made from clay, concrete and calcium silicate. Some types are stronger than others, a factor which is particularly important in areas where severe frost, extreme climatic variations or constant sea mist and spray are experienced. Suppliers and local authorities will be able to give further advice.

While most builders use newly made bricks, some people prefer the option of second-hand bricks which are well-weathered and lend an instantly aged and mellow character to the garden. These are not always easy to find although demolition or architectural salvage companies often have stocks.

Whatever you choose, it is important not to mix different types of brick in a single wall, unless each forms a separate skin (veneer). Concrete and clay bricks have a different rate of expansion and contraction which can lead to cracking if they are combined.

Facebricks (sometimes referred to as facing bricks) are attractive and durable. Clay facebricks are fired at a high temperature, making them strong and highly resistant to adverse weather conditions. There are numerous different types on the market, ranging from relatively smooth surfaces to rough rustic and rockface finishes. Colours, too, are varied, and you can usually find a hue which fits the general theme of an outdoor area. Concrete facebricks are also widely available and manufactured in a range of textures and colours.

Non-face bricks (non-facing bricks) are intended for general building work which is to be rendered (plastered). Since this type of brick is generally protected with rendered mortar, normal grades are not usually fired to the same temperature as facebricks. Non-face brick walls are sometimes left unrendered, to create a deliberate feeling of rusticity. If this is your aim, it is essential to check durability factors

Plants have been allowed to cascade over the edge of a dry stone retaining wall.

Common on sloping plots, retaining walls are invaluable for creating terraces and enlarging the functional area of any garden. They are also often essential where one property is higher than the adjacent one, or where it is necessary to cut into an embankment. Whilst it is quite acceptable to plant a slope (provided of course the gradient is not too steep), both activity and utility areas require a reasonably flat, level surface, and a retaining wall is often the answer.

As the name suggests, retaining walls are built to retain or restrain earth which would otherwise collapse. This means it is vital that the structure is able to resist the forces exerted by the retained material and any extra load which may be imposed on it. This includes everything from soil to buildings and even rain water.

Since even the lowest structure will have to hold a considerable volume of soil in place, drainage will be a vital consideration. If the earth behind any retaining wall becomes waterlogged,

the structure could collapse, irrespective of the method used to build it. If the wall is more than about 1.5 m high, you should always consult an engineer for advice or, possibly, plans. Unless the wall is less than 1 m to 1.2 m high, many local authorities will in any case require plans.

The layout of your house and garden, as well as the site itself, will determine where retaining walls (if any) are to be built, as well as the method of construction.

Various materials may be used, although the strongest and most suitable are probably limited to stone, concrete blocks (including specially designed modular retaining blocks) and clay bricks. Timber poles are sometimes used for very low walls, such as those found around flower beds, and reinforced concrete can be cast *in situ* to form some major, engineer-designed structures. These may be cantilevered, buttressed or, in the case of a gravity wall, built to such dimensions that it relies on its own mass for stability.

Apart from poles, the simplest type of

retaining wall is constructed with either interlinking or interlocking concrete blocks (see pages 51–53).

These are commonly laid so that they step backwards into the slope, although some designs create vertical walls and may incorporate steps, seating and flower boxes. Since these modular units are hollow, they are commonly filled with earth and then planted, to create what will eventually become a living wall.

The height of the wall will determine the type of foundations required. Low walls built with interlocking blocks may need no foundation other than well-compacted earth, but as a rule all masonry walls must be erected on proper concrete foundations. It is important that such walls should include weep holes or drainage pipes (which are sometimes perforated) at the base of the wall, and should be backfilled with free-draining material such as coarse aggregate to prevent soil from clogging the weep holes. Get professional advice for walls more than 1.5 m high.

Modular concrete retaining blocks.

A timber fence runs along the top of a high retaining wall built from stone.

A combination of wall and fence types.

A smoothly rendered brick wall looks neat and attractive and blends with most houses.

Natural stone, found in the area, was used to build this retaining wall within the garden.

Stone

The natural tones and texture of stone are hard to beat. Whether you opt for a random method of laying the material or use dressed stone, cut to form regularly shaped blocks, stone will add charm and character to the garden. Your choice of stone will depend largely on what is available locally. In rocky country, you may be able to use stone found on site; otherwise visit any nearby quarries and see what they have to offer. Other suppliers may be listed in a classified telephone directory (Yellow Pages). If you require a specific type of stone, you may have to get it from another area and could be faced with costly transport charges.

You will find that stone suitable for building is available in a wide range of colours and surface textures. Some, like granite, are extremely tough, making the material durable but difficult to cut. Limestone and sandstone are probably the easiest types to cut and trim, but this can be a disadvantage, especially in very cold or wet climates. Since soft stone will absorb moisture, it is best to coat the finished surface with a good quality masonry sealer.

Stone surfaces are classified according to their finish: polished stone (not usually chosen for garden work) is very smooth; rockfaced (split-faced) stone is rough; while picked, axed and split stone (as well as several other types) has a finished appearance somewhere between the two. For the purposes of garden work it is sufficient to think in broad terms of either dressed stone or rubble walls.

Dressed stone is cut or trimmed and finished to some degree, so that it can be laid in a reasonably regular fashion. Ashlar, which is square-hewn and smoothly finished, creates an imposing effect, while squared rubble will look more informal. Both are laid in uniform courses much the same way as bricks or blocks.

The joints of a dressed stone wall are pointed in a similar way to brickwork, and may be finished so they are more or less flush with the surface or

with your supplier first. The characteristic white saltiness of efflorescence may add the bucolic charm you want, but if the walls are likely to crumble after a few years, you will most definitely want to use a better quality product or to consider rendering the surface instead.

Rendered (plastered) walls

Both blocks and bricks (see pages 21 and 22) may be rendered (plastered) with a mortar mix of cement, building sand, possibly lime, and water (see page 35). There are several finishes and textures which can be achieved, but your choice will largely depend on existing finishes which have been applied to the exterior of your house and outbuildings.

An even finish can be achieved by smoothing the mortar with a wooden float. Very rough finishes can be created by spattering the render, using a simple hand-operated appliance, while a fairly crude Spanish-plaster effect can be produced by indenting the surface with a float.

rusticated to create a sunken joint. Unfortunately it has become very expensive to use cut stone, and skilled craftsmen may be quite difficult to locate in many areas. Furthermore, handling large stones can be extremely slow and heavy work.

Rubble walls are built with uncut or rough-cut stone which is laid in a random fashion. Shapes are varied and so rows are not at all regular. To add stability to the structure, it is wise to lay a flattish course about every 300 mm.

Cheaper to build than a dressed stone (ashlar) wall, but just as much hard work and effort, a rubble wall is characteristic of the traditional cottage-style garden.

Pebble and flint walls are less common, but nonetheless attractive. The shape of the material is irregular, and its size small, so it will not produce a particularly stable structure if used on its own. For this reason, bricks are usually incorporated as a foundation, at corners and as a capping. Steel-grey flint is not available everywhere, but it is possible to use similar pebbles to create the characteristic effect.

Dry stone walls, built without any mortar, are particularly attractive in a rural situation. There is, however, an art to building a dry wall, and it can be an extremely time-consuming project.

Freestanding dry walls must be built so that they slope inwards from the foundation on both sides. This so-called 'batter' is accomplished by making the base of the wall wider than the top. To ensure that it is stable and well balanced, this type of structure incorporates regular bond- or tie-stones which extend through the wall, from one face to the other. The two faces are built with large, heavy stones, usually with a space between them which is filled with chips or smaller stones and pebbles. It is also possible to fill the gap and pack the stones with earth, an especially useful method if you want to plant the wall.

Various cappings may be used to finish a dry wall, including upended stones which may be laid in several traditional patterns. Or you can top the structure with soil and plant it with herbs or ground cover.

Although a retaining dry stone wall is similar in structure, it slopes backwards, in one direction, towards the earth it is holding in place (see page 23).

Concrete

Made by mixing cement, sand and a suitable aggregate (crushed stone or coarse gravel) together with water, concrete may be precast in panels and then erected between upright posts, or used to construct freestanding or retaining walls *in situ*.

Cast (poured) concrete may be used to construct a wall of almost any size or configuration and, if properly reinforced, will provide an exceedingly strong structure. This method is particularly useful for retaining walls (see page 23), but the structure should be designed by an engineer if it is to exceed a height of 1.5 m.

Precast concrete walls are usually factory-made and supplied in panels which are erected horizontally between precast posts. Reasonably versatile, the panels are made in a range of patterns and textures, including brick-faced, smooth and pebbled finishes. Although not especially attractive, they are relatively inexpensive and are well suited for enclosing properties.

A disadvantage of precast concrete walls is that nails cannot be hammered directly into the material and so it is difficult to train creepers and climbers over the structure. An obvious solution is to place a timber trellis in front of the wall and to allow plants to cover this.

Timber

Although timber is more commonly used for fencing (see pages 26–27), walls (stockades) of wood are suitable

An interesting, freestanding dry stone wall has a charm associated with the countryside.

Precast panels on a cast concrete base.

Timber fencing creates a good, solid screen around a suburban property.

A low post-and-rail fence made with poles that have been painted white.

for retaining soil. Since this material is likely to deteriorate more rapidly than masonry or concrete, sturdy logs, poles or railway sleepers (ties) are the most suitable choice. The timber should always be treated with a suitable preservative, and preferably coated with bitumen or some other suitable waterproofing compound.

FENCES

There are many different types of fences to choose from, some of which are more solid and substantial, as well as more secure, than others. Fences are often categorised by the construction material used, and this is how they are listed here. However, a combination of elements may be found in a single structure: wooden poles may be used to support wire mesh, or timber panels may be set between precast concrete posts.

Timber

Both hardwoods (from broadleafed tree species) and softwoods (from conifers) may be used for fencing, although it is the less expensive timbers which are normally used. Your choice will depend to some extent on the wood available in your area. At the same time, the most popular types and styles of fence are universal. Some fences are made from sawn and planed (dressed) timber, others from rough or machined poles. In some instances it is quite acceptable to use wood with the bark still on it – this really depends on the effect you wish to achieve. Generally, rough surfaces will give a rustic look, while a smoother, better-finished appearance tends to seem more sophisticated.

Regardless of the look you want to achieve and the type of fence you decide to build, a golden rule is to use only sound, durable timber. If you use inferior materials, the structure is likely to deteriorate, or even collapse, within a relatively short time.

It is usually sensible to choose timber that has been pressure-treated in the factory, since the average DIY products do not penetrate the wood thoroughly. However the heartwood (found towards the centre of the tree) of some hardwoods is naturally resistant to infestation, so in areas where this is affordable, it is a particularly good choice for fencing posts. Unfortunately these hardy, decay-resistant species (red cedar, redwood and cypress are probably the best known) are not always readily available in all parts of the world.

Paling (palisade) and pole fences are versatile and relatively simple to erect. They do, however, require a lot of timber and therefore can be expensive. Stakes may either be pushed into the ground or nailed to a timber frame which is erected first. If poles (or even railway sleepers) are used, they are generally set in a concrete foundation to create the impression of a stockade.

Panel fences may be built with various materials, including PVC, but timber is undoubtedly the most common option. Prefabricated panels are widely available and are set between some kind of pillar or post, usually made from either precast concrete, timber or even bricks and mortar. Although these upright posts obviously must be strong enough to support the panels, no horizontal framework is normally necessary.

Not only are these fences relatively quick to erect, but they are also economical, and will create effective windbreaks and a solid barrier wherever these are required.

Where timber is used for panel fences, it is generally less substantial in section than the wood used for either post-and-board or picket fences (see below). This does mean, though, that it can be easily interwoven to create an attractive basketweave effect if desired. Exterior-grade plywood is another material which is popular in some parts of the world. Nailed to a frame which is then fixed to the posts, this material forms a solid screen which provides maximum privacy. Lattice panels, on the other hand, create a shield which offers some visual access beyond.

Picket fences are a perennial favourite in numerous settings. Particularly popular for creating a period feel or country-cottage look, pickets are nailed to horizontal rails which in turn are fixed to upright wooden posts. The framework may be assembled *in situ*, and the pickets nailed on to complete the fence; alternatively, picket panels may be attached to the posts as illustrated on pages 38–41. Although the majority of picket fences have straight or angled picket tops, there are many other possibilities, including spear and arrow shapes and even various simple but very effective cut-out designs. While some of the more intricate patterns require reasonably competent carpentry skills, for most people it just means a little more time and effort. Or you may choose to craft the top of the posts and to keep the pickets plain.

Post-and-rail fences may be made with poles, sawn timber, or even with stout square posts and matching rails. The simplest and probably the most common design entails connecting a double row of horizontal rails to short upright posts, set in the ground at equal intervals. The wood you choose, as well as the method used to build the fence, will determine its character. Machined poles used for both post and rail look neat and may even be painted white. Some companies will supply the required lengths with pre-cut holes which enable one to simply slot the poles together. Alternatively, round upright posts may be combined with split-pole rails, which are nailed into the adjoining timber. If the bark is still attached to the wood, the fence will have a more rustic appearance.

Post-and-board fences are usually similar to post-and-rail designs, except that they use sawn planks or board rather than rails. The most typical type incorporates three boards attached horizontally to either sawn posts or wooden poles. Variations involve adding additional timber horizontally or incorporating diagonal slats.

Of course, timber posts and boards may also be used to create a solid 'close-boarded' structure, in which case the boards are positioned closely together when they are nailed to the posts. Alternatively, slats may be set in place to create a series of either horizontal or vertical louvres.

Hurdles and brush fencing are less usual options in many areas, but are attractive and ideal for privacy. Hurdles are hand-crafted using traditional methods which involve weaving lengths of green, pliable wood to form rustic barriers and arches. Brush fencing is held in place with wire stretched between poles.

Bamboo and reeds
Both bamboo and river reeds may be used to create an effective screen or fencing. Mature bamboo, which resembles thick poles when dry, may be set in place to form a closely abutting palisade, while younger plants or river reeds may be tacked or tied onto a post-and-rail framework. Alternatively, these materials may be assembled into panels and then erected against supporting posts.

Unfortunately, even though these materials are attractive and well suited to screens and fences, they are not always available commercially and may be difficult to source. If there is not a natural supply in your area, you may also find this an expensive option.

The most suitable reeds are the Spanish or Norfolk varieties depending on availability. They should be stripped of their tough outer growth and cut to size before they dry out and become hard and brittle; when the reeds are green and pliable they are easier to work with and less likely to crack.

Several types of bamboo may be used, depending on the look you want to achieve. Mature, woody stems may be used to create an open fence effect, while those with thinner, cane-like branches may be tied together in the same way as reeds and are generally better suited for panels. Like reeds, this plant material does tend to become brittle as it dries out, so if you are nailing it in place, it is advisable to drill pilot holes to prevent splitting.

Metal and wire
Various types of metal and wire fencing may be used between posts of metal, timber or masonry. While wire is probably the most inexpensive option, wrought-ironwork can be the most decorative. Another possiblity is chain, which may be strung between

Poles are ideal for an all-weather fence.

A decorative metal railing is set on a wall.

It takes considerably longer to create a hedge than to construct a fence or build a wall. However, hedges are an inexpensive option for both boundaries and internal screens and offer an attractive alternative in many situations. Used for screening and enclosing gardens for centuries, hedges provide privacy and, once established, create an effective windbreak. They also add interest, colour and texture to the garden, filtering sunlight and introducing an element of contrast.

A hedge effect created by planting.

A wide selection of plants is suitable for hedging purposes, and many of these species will encourage birds to visit the garden – an added bonus, especially in an urban environment.

It is possible to plant either an informal or a formal hedge. The former is really just a densely planted row of plants intended to create a barrier or screen. An informal hedge requires a relatively large space to succeed, and since a variety of plants are usually included, these will invariably grow at different rates.

Formal hedges are also created by growing plants close together, but here the same species is grouped for effect and the foliage trimmed regularly to create a neat shape. This cutting back also encourages growth and makes the hedge thick and bushy, especially at the base.

A common error when trying to establish a hedge is to opt for fast-growing plants. They will certainly cover the area quickly, but will invariably outgrow the framework you intended them to fill at an equally rapid rate. It may be frustrating to wait several seasons for a hedge to establish itself, but it is usually worth it.

Suitable plants need to be severely cut back when they are young and the growing tips should be removed frequently during the growing season. This is because it is essential to prevent plants becoming 'leggy', lower growth being vital to the overall effect. Once the shape and form of the hedge has been established, the only major effort necessary is regular trimming, the frequency depending on the species.

The type and size of hedge you decide to plant will depend entirely on its location and function. A boundary hedge may be allowed to grow quite high, whilst a pretty lavender border around a herb garden will be small by comparison.

There are certain plants which are considered traditional hedging species. These include yew, box and the deciduous beech. Myrtle is a useful plant for low hedges and various Eugenias are very suitable for boundaries. Climatic conditions and the general availablity of plants in your area will be a major factor to consider. Any competent nurseryman will be able to advise on the best hedging plants for your area.

posts; however, this will simpy define a boundary without offering some security or privacy and so is not considered in any detail.

Barbed wire, sold in single strand rolls, is most commonly used for farm fencing or between extension arms erected in industrial situations. Check with your local authority before using this material around your home as there are restrictions in some areas (see also page 19).

Wire-mesh fencing is practical and utilitarian, as well as being relatively inexpensive. Even though it is not particularly attractive on its own, many people choose it because it is affordable and is easily covered with climbing and twining plants.

The mesh is attached to horizontal straining wires stretched between upright posts and intermediate standards, made of either precast concrete, tubular metal or timber (which all must be concreted into the ground). Thinner metal risers or timber poles may be used as standards.

There are various configurations of mesh fencing available, including square welded mesh, hexagonal wire netting and diamond mesh (chain link), usually manufactured with either a clinched, open-ended or barbed top. Relatively lightweight chicken wire (poultry fencing) is another inexpensive option, although it is not generally suitable for perimeter boundaries, being better suited for barricades within the garden itself.

As a precaution against rust, it is important to choose mesh which has been galvanised or coated with PVC. The most common coating is green, but it is sometimes possible to buy black, white or even various primary-coloured materials.

Metal fencing comes in various guises including ornamental wrought iron, modern grille-work and lightweight aluminium. Also made from metal is special swimming pool fencing, commonly manufactured with a hoop top or attractive roll top and minimal horizontal supports to prevent children from being able to climb it.

Perhaps the most attractive metal fencing is the traditional wrought-iron type reminiscent of the Victorian era. Usually incorporated between pillars and above a low brick or stone wall, these designs are now also widely available in aluminium.

More modern designs may also be included within a wall design

Whilst some metal is coated with PVC, other types may be painted or, if the metal is galvanised, left bare.

Almost all types of metal fencing are best erected by professionals or specialist companies.

Normally designed to provide partial protection or privacy within the garden, screens are a useful landscaping tool. Like conventional walls and fences, they may be erected for many reasons: to separate activity areas, to hide rubbish bins, washing lines and other service areas from view, to provide some protection from the sun and to shield specific parts of the garden from the wind. Some types are useful for supporting plants, whilst others will enable you to create an illusion of solitude. With some imagination, it is even possible to use simple screens to create the effect of an outdoor living room.

Even though most types of fence (see pages 26–28), and even some walls, may be used for screening, many people prefer less substantial structures which allow a glimpse of what lies beyond, and do not block the light. The fact that they are essentially small in scale and size also increases the range of possibilities. For instance, whilst it would be foolhardy to use glass or polycarbonate panels to fence off an entire area, these materials may be successfully used as a short screen alongside a patio or pool. Similarly, properly treated canvas or awning material (shadecloth) may be fixed to a wooden framework to create a screen, or you may be lucky enough to find some old wrought-ironwork or decorative fencing which could be used to good effect. Elaborate latticework, or even a straightforward trellis, is also better confined to relatively short lengths.

Relatively lightweight structures, including latticework screens and trellis panels, may be used to create a period feel or to provide a climbing frame for plants. Made of thin laths of wood which cross one another vertically and horizontally, or diagonally in a regular, crisscross pattern, they will provide an attractive partition which does not block out too much sunlight.

Prefabricated trellis panels are usually available in various sizes. Alternatively, you can make your own structure, spacing the laths as close together or far apart as you wish. Latticework, which is predominantly a decorative feature, benefits from the addition of posts and finials, while trellis is planted.

Fencing, as already stated, is not always suitable for screening purposes, but a fairly low picket fence could be used

Several wooden screens shield areas of the garden and provide frames for plants.

very successfully in some instances, particularly if it is decoratively finished. Alternatively a bamboo palisade or pole fence might be an option. Where there is a need for a good windbreak or a structure to buffer noise, most solid timber fencing types (especially board and panel designs) could be used.

Walls are sometimes used for screening, particularly around entertainment patios or other activity areas which need some protection from the elements. However, consider the effects of wind before constructing a solid wall: staggered bricks or perforated screen (breeze) blocks are often a more practical option. For something different, glass bricks may be used on a small scale, or they may be combined with conventional building blocks.

Ultimately, your choice will depend on personal preference and lifestyle, the function your screen will fulfil and the site where it is to be constructed.

Latticework between precast pillars.

A club hammer is useful for knocking standards for wire-mesh fencing into the ground.

It is important to keep fencing straight and to ensure that all corners are at right-angles.

Careful planning and a thorough understanding of correct building methods are essential for anyone planning to tackle their own walls and fences. Whilst the basic principles are quite elementary, if you want a professional result it is necessary to practise the techniques involved. In addition, a newcomer to DIY will have to ensure that he or she is properly equipped with the correct tools.

There are only a handful of basic rules and these apply to all building methods, irrespective of the materials used: you need a reliable design, good quality materials, and the right tools for the job. But even more important is the need to keep all structures square, level and plumb.

BASIC PRINCIPLES

It should come as no surprise that essential building principles are based on common sense. After all, if a wall is not level, and the corners of a fence are not accurately angled, there will be a danger that these structures will collapse. Unless a wall or fence is curved, it will always be square, level and plumb. Even if a fence is to follow contours, the posts must be upright and straight; and if a wall is to be curved, both horizontal and vertical planes must still be kept level. Although this may be a little more difficult with a material like natural stone, these fundamental principles must be adhered to.

Square

For any structure to be absolutely square, the corners must form 90°. This means that foundations, the footings for pillars, brick courses and so on should all be checked for accuracy at frequent intervals during the building programme.

There are several ways of checking for square, the simplest being to use a tool made for this purpose. A steel builders' square is useful for setting out projects and for bricklaying, while a smaller combination or adjustable carpenters' square is ideal for any woodwork project.

The 3:4:5 method is an invaluable aid in ensuring that walls and fences have been correctly set out: measure 3 m and 4 m respectively out from a central point to form a right angle; then measure the distance between the endpoints of these two lines – it should equal 5 m. If it does not, adjust the angle of the two lines until you get 5 m; at this point, the angle will be 90°.

Level and plumb

Although you may want to create a slight gradient for drainage purposes, most surfaces will need to be level. It is essential to check the levels regularly, from the foundations up. Poles and posts must be perfectly vertical and brickwork must be both level and plumb. If a wall begins to lean out of alignment, this must be rectified immediately.

The most common tool used for this purpose is an ordinary spirit level. When this is placed against any surface, the bubble in the vial should be centred. A line level, which is simply a spirit vial on a line, may be used to check the horizontal plane of brickwork. Many spirit levels have both horizontal and vertical vials and are invaluable aids for checking vertical planes (plumb).

A combination square (which also incorporates a spirit vial) is useful for ensuring that timber is properly aligned. Invaluable for setting out walls and fences on sloping ground, and for checking that posts and poles are the same height, a water level is also one of the cheapest tools available. The concept that water finds its own level is a simple one and the technique of using it is easy to master: all you need is a length of transparent tubing, or two short pieces of tubing inserted into either end of a length of garden hose. Once filled with water, the tubing is attached to a post or held by a helper at a given point, and the other end moved to the position you want to be the same level. Although not essential

A steel builders' square is invaluable for checking angles when setting out foundations.

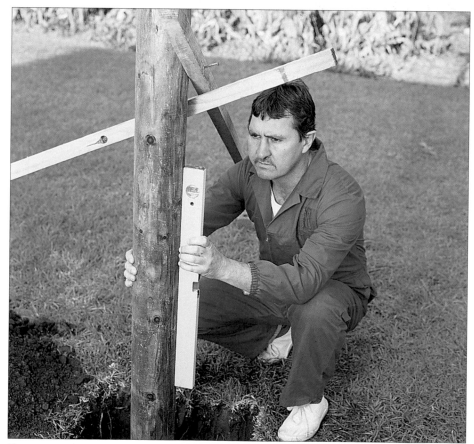

Use a spirit level to ensure that all posts and upright poles are perfectly vertical.

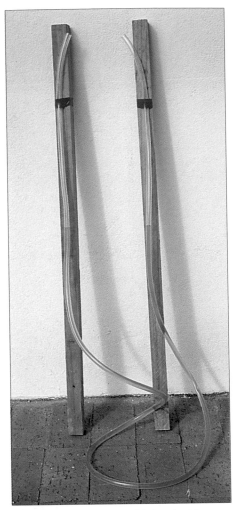

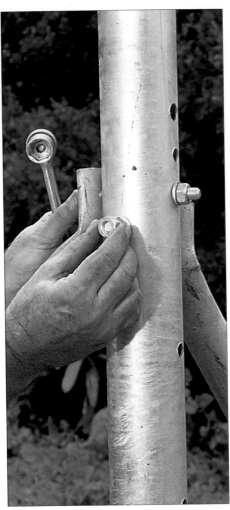

A homemade water level is invaluable.

Use a spanner to tighten nuts and bolts.

in the tool kit, a plumb bob may be used to check that brickwork is vertical. More commonly used as a final check, the simplest plumb bob is attached to a piece of string; more expensive ones have a built-in line reel.

THE TOOL KIT

It is not necessary to purchase an expensive tool kit to erect a fence or build a wall. In fact, a lot of DIY enthusiasts have most of the essential tools, including spades and shovels, a retractable tape measure, spirit level, screwdrivers, drill and builders' square (see page 30–31). If you do not have a spiral ratchet screwdriver, with different positions and a reverse action enabling you to remove screws easily, consider adding this to your tool kit.

For brickwork you will need a bricklaying trowel for spreading mortar, and a plasterer's wooden float if you are planning to render the surface. Both homemade corner blocks and metal line pins are invaluable aids for keeping brick courses straight and level. Although they are sometimes available commercially, corner blocks are simple to make from blocks of wood. Exact dimensions are not important, but you will need to create two L-shaped pieces of wood with a groove through the centre of each foot of the L. Once builders' line or string has been wound through the slots and around the feet, the blocks may be slotted onto the brickwork at either end, so that the string is in line with the next brick or block course.

Another useful tool, easily made, is a gauge rod: this is a straight-edged piece of timber marked off to indicate each brick course plus mortar joints of 10–15 mm.

A rubber mallet or a club hammer is useful (although not essential) for knocking blocks into place, as is a brick hammer or bolster chisel (used with a club hammer) for the rough cutting of bricks and blocks. You may also need an angle grinder in order to cut concrete blocks accurately.

For timber fencing you will need, as well as some of the above, a suitable handsaw or an electric saw. A general

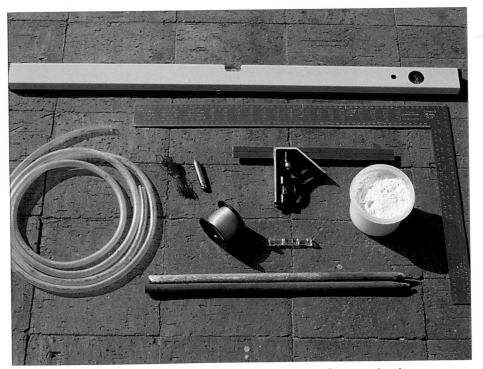

The essential tools required for setting out and ensuring all surfaces are level.

purpose bowsaw is useful for cutting poles, while a tenon saw is invaluable for trimming small pieces of wood. A jigsaw, which may be used to create curves and angles, is an ideal electric saw to buy, although a circular saw is a better choice if large pieces of timber are to be cut. Clamps are also a useful addition to your tool kit. Useful types include common G-clamps, corner clamps (useful when joining timber at right angles) and sash clamps (to hold long pieces of timber in place).

Spanners or wrenches will be required to tighten nuts and bolts on some types of fencing (see page 42), and fencing pliers or a wire strainer to tension a wire-mesh fence.

Power tools will make your job much easier. In addition to a saw, you will find that an electric (or even a battery-operated) drill is an indispensable aid for many projects. Ideally, invest in a machine that has adjustable speeds.

Although concrete may be mixed by hand, many people prefer to use a concrete mixer which may be electrically powered or driven by petrol or diesel. Available in various sizes, these machines may be hired.

While a portable work-bench is useful, a table or trestles may be used to assemble timber panels or pickets.

FOUNDATIONS

The importance of a solid foundation cannot be underestimated. While not all walls need to be laid on concrete, and not all fencing posts need to be embedded in a concrete footing, it is only the smaller and lower structures which may be erected or constructed without concrete.

The size, depth and type of footings or foundations will depend on the design of the wall or the kind of fencing you plan to erect, as well as soil conditions in your garden. Minimum dimensions will usually be specified in your local building regulations. If you are uncertain of the correct options, consult a professional.

The mass of any structure is spread over the width of the foundation. If the soil is unstable, it is usually necessary to make the foundations wider.

There are various kinds of footings and foundations in the building industry, but freestanding garden walls are almost always built on a strip foundation. For this you will need to excavate a trench for the concrete. If the ground slopes, the trench must be stepped down, so that each level is flat.

As a rule, the trench should be at least 100 mm deep for a wall no more than 800 mm high, and 150–200 mm for higher walls. The foundation must be wider than the brick- or blockwork; an easy way to calculate the width of the foundation is to add the width of the wall to double the depth of the foundation. For instance, if a 220 mm-wide one-brick wall is built on a 150 mm-deep foundation, the foundation should be 520 mm wide.

The footings for a freestanding brick pillar measuring about 400 mm x 400 mm must be at least 200 mm deep and 200 mm wider than the pillar on all sides. Precast concrete pillars may be set on fairly thin footings, whilst posts and poles will need to be embedded in the ground, preferably in concrete, to stabilise them.

A safe rule of thumb when estimating footings for posts of all materials is to allow for a depth which equals a quarter of the full length. This means that you should buy 1.6 m-long poles for a 1.2 m-high fence, and 2.65 m-long poles for a 2 m-high fence.

Ideally, posts should be encased in concrete. This does not mean that the entire footing needs to be filled with concrete, though; some people fill about half with hardcore (broken bricks, stones and so on) and then top the hole with concrete; others anchor the base of the post in concrete and then fill the top with soil.

If a concrete footing is not provided for poles, the soil around the poles must be well compacted. In this case, it is often best to bury a longer length to ensure it is properly anchored.

Where they are available, fence spikes are an option which simplifies the job. Manufactured in several sizes, the spikes are welded to a square metal socket designed to anchor posts securely. As these are driven into the ground with a heavy sledge hammer, it can be a little difficult ensuring they

Measure the width of the foundation and string a line as a guide before you dig the trench.

Stretcher bond brickwork with drainage.

Well-bonded reconstituted concrete blocks.

are absolutely vertical. Use an offcut of wood in the socket to check for plumb before you have hammered the fence spike right into the ground.

Concrete

Made by mixing together various quantities of cement, sand and crushed stone (aggregate) with water, concrete hardens as a result of a chemical reaction that occurs between the cement and the water. Although it gains most of its strength within the first 28 days of being laid, concrete in moist soil will continue to strengthen for several years.

Although there are various types of cement, ordinary Portland cement is most commonly used. Sold in sacks, it should be stored in a dry place where it will not get hard and lumpy.

The sand used for concrete should be reasonably coarse (or sharp) compared to the soft building sand used for mortar. Although some builder's merchants sell it in bags, it is usually more sensible to order in bulk, even though the smallest load most suppliers will deliver is 0.5 m³.

Crushed stone (aggregate) is sold in bags or delivered in bulk. Gradings vary, but 19–20 mm 'single-sized' stone is most commonly used.

Various concrete mixes are recommended, depending on local conditions and the type of work which is to be done. In areas where good quality crushed stone is available, a 1:3:6 mixture (cement:sand:stone) is quite adequate for lightly loaded footings and the foundations of garden walls. If a relatively inferior 19 mm crushed stone is used, a ratio of 1:4:4 is preferred. If a stronger mix is required, alter the ratio to 1:2½:3½. Remember that the more sand you include in the mix, the weaker the concrete will be.

Concrete is always mixed in batches, depending on how much you can place before it begins to set. Mix it on a clean, dry surface or in a wheelbarrow. Measure the dry materials out in the preferred ratio, using a suitable container (a clean 25 litre paint drum is a good option).

Mix together the cement and sand until the colour of the mixture is fairly uniform. Form a hollow in the middle, and then add a little water at a time (being careful not to make the mixture too sloppy), gradually mixing by shovelling the dry materials into the middle. When you have a workable consistency, add the crushed stone. If it seems dry, add a little more water.

When using a concrete mixer, it is advisable to load the crushed stone into the mixer first. This will help prevent a build-up of cement on the blades. Then add the cement, sand and enough water to blend it together.

It is vital that the concrete does not dry out before it is placed. Also, if the stone begins to settle, you will need to mix it again. Although the concrete should not be placed on saturated ground where water has pooled, it is good building practice to lightly wet the sub-base to prevent the soil from absorbing moisture from the concrete.

Unless the upper level of your foundation or footing will be above ground level for some reason, it is not necessary to construct formwork to hold the concrete in place. You can pour or shovel it into the excavated trench and then compact it well by tamping with the back of a shovel (or, for smaller jobs, even with the trowel). You can also use a straight-edged piece of wood to smooth the surface, using a chopping action to further compact it and expel air bubbles, and a sawing action to level it. Remember that where reinforcing is included, it is essential to compact the concrete thoroughly to minimise voids.

Concrete must be kept moist for it to cure, and ideally it should be left for five to seven days before building commences. In practice, though, most builders start brickwork the day after the foundations are complete.

BRICKLAYING

While the technique of laying bricks and blocks is well illustrated in the step-by-step instructions that follow, note that success lies in the basic principles previously mentioned: unless a wall is square, level and plumb, it will not look professional.

It is important to use a suitable mortar mix (see pages 44 and 48). The mortar is mixed in much the same way as concrete, but without the addition of stone (cement:sand in a 1:4 ratio, or weaker if required). You need clean builders' sand (preferably soft sand) for the mixture. Good quality building sand is evenly graded. Avoid sand with clay in it or any sand which contains salt or shell particles. Lime may be added to the mixture to improve workability, or use a proprietary plasticiser in the quantities recommended by the manufacturer. It is best to mix reasonably small batches of mortar, especially if you are not an experienced bricklayer.

Each course of bricks or blocks is bedded in mortar, while the end of every brick or block to be laid is 'buttered' by squashing the mortar onto it. Each one is pushed firmly into position and then gently tapped with the handle of the trowel to level it. If there is still a gap between bricks or blocks, this is filled afterwards with more mortar using a trowel. It pays to work neatly, and excess mortar should be scraped from the wall as you work.

Do not forget that you will need to check all your surfaces regularly with a spirit level to ensure they are level. Corner blocks and a line (see page 32) will help keep courses straight, and a gauge rod will enable you to check that mortar joints are even.

RENDERING (PLASTERING)

There are two reasons for rendering walls with mortar: aesthetics and to make them more weatherproof.

For a successful job, it is essential that the mortar sticks to the surface you are rendering. It must also cure without cracking. A newly built wall will usually be suitable for rendering; an old wall may need to be cleaned to ensure that it is free of dirt, dust and grime. Wet the surface just before work is to begin.

Before you start, you will need to estimate what quantities of cement and sand, and possibly lime, are required. A standard mixture comprises 50 kg cement, 25 kg lime and 250 kg of sand (1:½:5). Experts also recommend that the mortar used for block- or bricklaying should match that used to render the surface (see pages 44 and 48).

To help prevent cracking, avoid working in hot sun or strong wind. Mix small batches that can be used within an hour, and lay the mortar firmly on the wall with a plasterer's trowel. The mixture should not be thicker than 15 mm, or thinner than 10 mm.

You will need to leave the mortar to set for about an hour before scraping the surface with a screed board or straight-edged piece of wood. Then wood float it to get a reasonably smooth surface. If you want a rough surface, this can be achieved by brushing with a block brush instead of scraping and floating.

If the wall is very smooth, and the mixture does not adhere at first, you may need to apply a spatterdash coat to roughen the surface. This is done by mixing a thick slurry of cement and sand in the ratio 1:2, which is then spattered unevenly onto the wall surface. It should be kept moist with plastic sheeting or sacking until it sets properly, and you can then continue to render the wall.

Make sure that the rendered surface does not dry out too quickly. Try to keep it damp for two or three days by spraying it gently with a hosepipe, being careful to use a fine mist which will not damage the surface.

DRAINAGE

It is important to ensure that walls and fences do not become waterlogged. This is especially important for a retaining wall, which can act as a dam for any water which builds up behind it.

The simplest solution is to leave some of the vertical joints in the first course unmortared to create weep holes. Alternatively, incorporate a 40 mm drain pipe in the base of the wall at 600 mm intervals.

To improve the flow of water to the drain pipes, backfill the area behind the wall with gravel or crushed stone. It may also be advisable (if, for instance, clay is a problem) to include perforated pipework and a layer of geotextile material to form a fin-shaped drain which will allow the water to flow freely.

To prevent the wall face becoming stained with dissolved minerals, insert a vertical polythene damp course against the wall before backfilling.

Stormwater drains may also be necessary at the upper level of a retaining wall to aid the discharge of surface water which could otherwise cause the collapse of the wall.

An effective, fin-shaped drain is created with perforated piping and geotextile material.

Armed with a thorough knowledge of correct building principles, you should be confident enough to tackle most fence and wall projects. Many of the basic techniques are covered on pages 30–35, while more specific information and detailed instructions are given in the step-by-step instructions which follow. These illustrated guidelines range from the erection of a straightforward wire-mesh fence (which requires minimal building skills) to the construction of a relatively ambitious concrete block wall. The intention is to demonstrate a range of skills which will enable you to undertake any of the plan projects on pages 54–63, or even to devise and construct your own fence or wall design and layout.

There are step-by-step instructions for two types of timber structure: a very basic lattice screen, and a rather unusual picket fence which demonstrates how to assemble a standard panel and could easily be adapted for any other panel fence. The picket fence guidelines also clearly illustrate how to set out any wall or fence structure and include a thorough description of the 3:4:5 method explained on page 31. The importance of keeping all posts vertical is also emphasised photographically.

While the step-by-step instructions for a wire-mesh fence are reasonably basic, they also detail how to tension the material correctly and how to use fencing pliers to neatly finish the job. Although the uprights used here are tubular galvanised metal poles, any type of suitable posts and standards may be used. Instructions are included in the box on page 42 for ordinary metal droppers and for timber poles, either of which may be incorporated.

In an effort to illustrate a good cross-section of wall types, the step-by-step instructions include a reasonably wide range of materials and possibilities. Additional information about bricks, blocks, foundations and mortar requirements is included, where relevant, in the introductory section to each set of guidelines. Again, the intention is that the instructions will enable you to tackle any type or design of wall you may wish to build.

Several possibilities are given in the plans on pages 54–63.

Basic bricklaying skills are illustrated in the step-by-step facebrick wall shown on pages 44–45. Facebricks were used here to build a one-brick (double skin) wall which includes a simple pillar which could be used to hang a gate. One would use the same techniques for all other brick types.

The reconstituted stone wall, also with pillars, illustrates how different-sized units are incorporated in a single structure, as well as how to lay capping along the top of a wall, while the concrete block wall features a rubbish bin compartment and a doorway. There are also step-by-step instructions for rendering (plastering) the concrete block wall.

The final set of instructions illustrates the basic methods used to construct retaining walls with concrete modular blocks and with smaller terrace blocks.

You could also build a retaining wall with bricks or concrete blocks and mortar, provided adequate steps are taken to ensure there is proper drainage (see page 35).

ESTIMATING QUANTITIES

BRICKS AND BLOCKS

To build a single (half-brick) wall use 55 bricks for 1 m²
To build a double (one-brick) wall use 110 bricks for 1 m²
To build a wall with 390 mm x 190 mm x 190 mm blocks use
  12½ blocks for 1 m², and 100 blocks for 8 m²
To build a wall with 290 mm x 290 mm x 90 mm/100 mm
  perforated screen blocks use 11 blocks for 1 m²
To build a wall with any other blocks divide the surface area of the
  wall by the area of one block

CONCRETE MIXES

Quantities based on using 19–20 mm crushed stone
For lightly loaded footings use
  1 cement + 3 sand + 6 aggregate, or
  1 cement + 4 sand + 4 crushed stone
For heavy-duty foundations use
  1 cement + 2½ sand + 3½ aggregate, or
  1 cement + 3 sand + 3 crushed stone

CONCRETE

For a 1:3:6 mix use 220 kg cement for 1 m³
For a 1:4:4 mix use 250 kg cement for 1 m³
For a 1:2½:3½ mix use 300 kg cement for 1 m³
For a 1:3:3 mix use 320 kg cement for 1 m³

MORTAR MIXES

For laying facebricks use 1 cement + ½ lime (optional) + 4 sand
For concrete blockwork and non-facebricks use
  1 cement + ½ lime (optional) + 6 sand
For rendering (plastering) use as for above, or
  1 cement + ½ lime + 5 sand

MORTAR

To build a single (half-brick) wall use 50 kg cement for 200 bricks
To build a double (one-brick) wall use 50 kg cement for 150 bricks
To build a wall with 390 mm x 190 mm x 190 mm blocks use
  32½ kg cement to lay 100 blocks

Assembling a simple lattice panel, consisting of laths of wood which crisscross one another vertically and horizontally, or diagonally, takes very basic carpentry skills which are limited to sawing the wood and possibly drilling holes for bolts. You may, of course, choose to make several panels, and to mount them to a series of upright posts in the same way as for the picket fence, illustrated on pages 38–41. Since these structures are intended to be relatively lightweight,

very slim timbers may be used. If, however, you intend nailing each piece where it intersects the next, you will need to opt for laths which are thick enough to accommodate the nails. Your choice will depend on the design and reason for building the screen: if it is to form a trellis for plants, the wood must be strong enough to support climbers and creepers; if it is simply going to block an unsightly view, you can use thinner wood, but you may want to place the slats closer together.

MATERIALS

This screen uses thin 2.2 m x 44 mm x 10 mm laths attached at 144 mm centres to a 2.06 m x 1.63 m frame made with 44 mm x 44 mm battens. The completed screen is bolted to fairly hefty 2.25 m x 96 mm x 70 mm upright posts, one of which is bolted to the wall. If your screen is freestanding, anchor the posts in a concrete footing (see pages 33–34): the posts should then be 2.75–3.45 m long. You need 8 x 100 mm and 54 x 25 mm wire nails.

1 Cut the wood for the framework and laths to size with a tenon saw. For this design, cut 15 x 44 mm x 10 mm laths to a length of 1.63 m and 10 to a length of 2.06 m. Trim the 44 mm x 44 mm battens to make 2 x 1.63 m and 2 x 1.97 m lengths.

2 Assemble the lattice panel flat on the ground. Clamp the 44 mm x 44 mm lengths of timber at 90° with the longer lengths on the inside. Use a builder's square to check the angles. Nail together with two 100 mm-long wire nails at each angle.

3 Once the framework is complete, nail the 15 x 1.63 m horizontal laths into place at 100 mm intervals with 25 mm nails, placing a lath at each end to cover the frame. Nail on the 10 vertical laths, omitting the end lath on each side.

4 Bolt or concrete the upright posts into position, depending on the location you have chosen. Make sure they are correctly spaced and absolutely vertical. Position the latticework panel, using a spirit level to check for accuracy.

5 Now nail the panel to the upright posts, taking care not to shift it out of alignment. Alternatively, screw the panel into place, predrilling the holes. If the posts are a little longer than required, use a handsaw to cut the excess off the tops.

6 Finally, seal or paint the screen, or give it a coating of a penetrating oil dressing to preserve the wood. If you plan to grow plants over the screen, it is important to do this now, as the wood will be inaccessible once the plants have grown.

Picket fences are relatively simple to erect and yet, if they are imaginatively designed, they are one of the most attractive fencing possibilities available. Although they are traditionally quite low, picket fences may be built to any height. Similarly, while the typical kind features pickets that are fairly widely spaced, there is no reason why you should not attach them close together to gain privacy.

Made with posts and intermediate lengths of timber (or pickets) which are vertically attached to horizontal supports, these fences are sometimes sold in pre-assembled form.

If you are planning to make your own picket fence from scratch, it is essential to ensure that all the sections (or panels) between the posts are of equal length and that the pickets are all exactly the same size and height. The tops of the posts may be plain or decorative, and either sawn and planed timber or machined poles may be used, depending on the design.

The range of possibilities for pickets is endless, ranging from flat, rounded or pointed ends to intricate cut-outs or spear-shapes. The pickets shown in this step-by-step illustrate an ingenious method of creating the effect of a triangular cut-out. No special carpentry skills are necessary, and the only tool you will need is a jigsaw.

MATERIALS

Sawn and planed timber is used for this 1.2 m-high picket fence. There is no need to use timber of exactly the same dimension as shown here, but choose something similar. Most timber merchants use nominal sizes when describing the material; these relate to the original dimensions of the timber. When it is sawn there is some wastage, and even more once it has been planed.

Fairly stocky 100 mm x 40 mm upright posts are used here, while the 2.4 m horizontal support beams are 45 mm x 45 mm. You could also use 38 mm x 38 mm battens. The 1.2 m-high pickets are 70 mm x 18 mm in size. These pickets are made from 2.4 m lengths of timber, which are sawn in half at the correct angle.

The spacing of the pickets depends upon personal choice. The ones shown here are attached in pairs, because of the design. The space between the pickets alternates between 30 mm and 70 mm. You can alter this spacing if you wish, but remember that if you decrease it a greater number of pickets will be required for each panel.

FOOTINGS

Although the footings of a very low picket fence may be anchored directly in the ground, it is best to concrete them into place. The recommended ratio of cement:sand:crushed stone is 1:4:4. If you are using a really good quality crushed stone, you may alter this to 1:3:6. A stronger mix is not necessary for a fence of this height.

FIXING AND FASTENING

Galvanised nails should be used for all outdoor woodwork. Screws should either be galvanised or made of brass. Always choose nails and screws that will penetrate one piece of wood and go half to three-quarters of the way through the other.

Nails used to fix the slats to the support pieces are 50 mm long, while those used to nail the panels to the thicker posts are 75 mm long. Since a gate will be used often, it is best to use screws to fasten the timber; you need No. 6 (3.5 mm) x 35 mm-long screws for the Z-brace, and No. 6 (3.5 mm) x 16 mm screws for the hinges.

1 Mark out the position of the fence, hammering in pegs to indicate where the main supporting posts will be concreted into the ground. The distance between the posts will depend on the size of the picket panels (these are 2.4 m apart).

2 It is essential that you mark out the fence accurately. Measure the distance required between the pegs with a retractable steel rule, then string a line along the entire length to ensure that all the posts will be properly aligned.

3 Make certain that all corners are at 90°. The best way to check this is to use the 3:4:5 method (see page 31): measure and mark 300 mm and 400 mm on each side of the corner; the distance between the two should be 500 mm.

4 The wooden pegs mark the central position of each 400 mm x 400 mm footing. Since you will have to remove the pegs to excavate holes for the foundation footings, mark the area around each peg using cement, lime or even flour.

5 Remove the pegs and excavate each hole to a depth of about 400 mm, depending on the length of the posts. If the fence is to be erected in an area where there is established lawn, remove the sods of grass carefully so they can be re-used.

6 Use a steel tape to check that all the footings are the same depth as each other. Remember that each footing should be as deep as about a quarter of the total length of the posts, to ensure that the posts will be firmly anchored.

7 Timber which is to be buried in the ground should be given some extra protection, even if it has been previously treated. Coat the ends with creosote (although this is a toxic material) or with a bitumen waterproofing compound.

8 Now position all the upright posts in the footings, using battens or other suitable offcuts of timber to brace them firmly in place and keep them straight. Use a spirit level to ensure that each one of the posts is absolutely vertical.

9 You will need to make certain that the tops of all the posts are at the same height. Any longer ones will have to be trimmed, or dug deeper into the ground. Use a water level, and mark the top of the corner posts at the point where they are equal.

10 Tie a length of string tightly between each pair of corner posts at the height of the marks made in step 9. Use the string as a guide to mark this point on the other posts. Trim longer posts or dig deeper footings to make the tops of all posts level.

11 Now assemble the picket panels. Cut the tops of each picket to the required shape. These are to be cut at an angle, so use a carpenter's or combination square to mark an accurate cutting line, and cut all the tops at precisely the same angle.

12 Working on a portable work-bench or on a secure pair of trestles, use a jigsaw to cut across the line you marked. Each picket is 1.2 m high from the tip to base; and you will need 20 for each panel. Hold the wood steady and cut firmly.

13 Make triangular side-cuts in the upper section of each picket for a cut-out effect. Make sure that the cuts are at the same angles and the same distance from the top. Cut out with a jigsaw. When a pair of pickets is placed together it will form a diamond.

14 Each of the panels is 2.4 m long and is made by nailing 19 of the 20 pickets to two horizontal lengths of timber. It is vital that each of these horizontal lengths is exactly the same: measure them all and cut off the excess with a jigsaw or tenon saw.

15 The first picket of each slat is not attached until the panels have been nailed to the upright posts. Before assembling the panel, measure and mark the position of the second picket, 100 mm from the end, and the position of the last picket, 70 mm in.

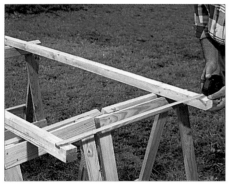

16 Place the two lengths of timber which will form the horizontal support beams for the pickets onto a working surface 800 mm apart, measuring this distance from the outer edge of each beam. Make sure they are equidistant along the full length.

17 Place the first picket across the two pieces of timber so that 200 mm extends above it and 200 mm below. Use a builder's square to make absolutely certain the picket meets the horizontal support beams at 90°, or the fence will not be square.

18 Nail the picket onto the horizontal beams. Use two galvanised nails (that will not rust outdoors) top and bottom and make sure that they are long enough to go through the picket as well as three-quarters of the beam.

19 You will need to space the pickets accurately, and the best way to do this is with straight lengths of timber. Here each pair of pickets is spaced with a 30 mm-wide batten, and every second one with a 70 mm-wide plank the same width as a picket.

20 Once all 19 pickets have been nailed in place, fix the panel to the upright posts. The panel must be positioned so that it is absolutely straight and the horizontal timbers level. If the ground slopes, support that section of the base with wood.

21 Although it is not necessary to screw any of the panels into place, it is sensible to drill pilot holes to prevent the wood from splitting when you nail the panels to the posts. Make sure that the size of the drill bit is narrower than the nails.

22 Hammer one nail into each horizontal section at each end. Note that the bracing timbers are still in position and that the posts have not yet been concreted into the ground. This enables you to adjust the panels to keep them in a totally straight line.

23 The number of panels required will depend on the total length of your fence. Position and nail all the panels, remembering to use a spirit level to check each one. Then nail on the missing picket at the beginning of each of the panels.

24 Before you concrete the posts into the ground, make sure the panels are aligned and use a spirit level to double-check that each post is still vertical. If any of them have moved, adjust the bracing otherwise you will end up with a skew fence.

25 On a clean, dry surface or in a wheelbarrow, mix the concrete in the ratio 1:4:4 (cement:sand:stone) or stronger if you wish (see page 34). Slightly dampen the soil in the holes before adding the cement, to prevent moisture being absorbed from the soil.

26 The 900 mm-wide gate is made in much the same way as the panels, except that only 8 pickets are used and these are held together with a sturdy Z-brace. This is made with 110 mm x 22 mm timber screwed securely to the pickets.

27 You will need to use gate hinges to attach the gate securely to the upright posts. Each hinge is screwed to the Z-brace. Use a wood bit to drill the holes and then secure the hinge with either galvanised or brass screws which will not rust.

28 Before you attach the gate it is vital to ensure that it is properly positioned. As it will not touch the ground, you will have to prop it up on several offcuts of wood. If the ground slopes, you will need to use more pieces on one side.

29 Use your spirit level vertically to check that the gate is straight. Then check again, placing the tool on the horizontal sections of the Z-brace to make sure that it is level. It is important to check carefully, as if it is not level the gate will hang at an angle.

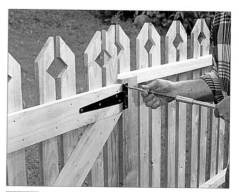

30 Mark the position of the hinges on the upright posts so that you can see where to drill holes in the posts. Remove the gate while drilling. Reposition it, then loosely position all 6 screws and tighten them gradually. Finally, fit a latch.

Wire mesh is the most inexpensive option when it comes to fencing. No complicated building skills are required, but it is essential to strain the wire correctly and to connect the mesh to the posts and straining wire neatly, using the proper tools.

If wire mesh is not properly strained, it will sag; all posts must be securely anchored in 600 mm-deep footings, filled at least halfway with concrete.

Intermediate standards can usually be set in 400 mm-deep footings.

Several types of corner and straining posts may be used (see box below). These are usually spaced up to 9 m apart, with standards set in the ground no less than every 3.5 m.

If there is a change in ground level along the length of the fence, an additional straining post will be required here.

MATERIALS

The step-by-step instructions show tubular metal posts (76 mm diameter at the corners and 48 mm in between). The PVC-coated 2.5 mm diamond (chainlink) mesh is strained with 3 mm wire, while thinner 2 mm wire is used to bind it to the post.

You will need 3 horizontal rows of straining wire for a 1.2 m-high fence, and 4 if it is 1.8 m high.

UPRIGHT SUPPORTS

Droppers (stakes)
Ordinary droppers are a reasonably cheap option, and are simply hammered into place. Thread binding wire through the holes and use fencing pliers to twist it around the straining wire.

Timber poles
Timber poles are easily included in a wire-mesh fence, even if metal corner posts are used. They are concreted into position. Hammer in 2–3 U-shaped fencing staples to connect the strainers to the poles.

Galvanised metal poles
These are concreted firmly into the ground. They are connected to the strainers with thinner straining wire. It is essential that holes for the wires are drilled before the posts are concreted into place.

1 Tubular metal corner and straining posts are usually assembled before they are concreted into place. Bolt the stays to the uprights using the correct spanners. If wooden posts and stays are used, these can be nailed together.

2 Before any posts are set in the ground, you will have to decide exactly where the fence is to be erected. Set out the line it is to follow and then mark out the position of all corner posts. Mark the footings and then excavate to the required depth.

3 Intermediate standards must be placed in line with the corner posts. Use the 3:4:5 method (see page 31) to ensure that the line you are following is at 90° to the first corner post, and then measure and mark the position of the other uprights.

4 Once the upright posts and stays are in place, check that the post is vertical. Fill the footings at least halfway with concrete and top them with soil. Leave the footings to set overnight and then attach the straining wires.

5 Insert suitable eye bolts (straining bolts) into the holes in the top of the corner posts, together with nuts and washers. Do not tighten the bolt completely; turn the nut gently until the bolt just appears through the back of the nut.

6 Measure enough of the straining wire to span the posts plus a little extra to enable you to wind it tightly to the posts at each end. Cut the wire with a pair of proper fencing pliers, using the correct slot to get a good, clean break.

7 Loop the wire through the eye of the straining bolt and use the groove in the front of the fencing pliers to hold it taut. Now secure the wire by twisting it back around itself, so that it does not slip back through the bolt when you start to strain the full length.

8 Tighten the nut with a spanner, using a screwdriver to stop the bolt from turning. Do not tighten either side completely; rather take up the slack gradually from both ends. It is best to tighten the bottom wire first before tightening those above it.

9 Using a screwdriver to help hold the bolt secure, use the specially designed underside of the fencing pliers (between the handles) to wind the wire neatly back around itself. Trim the excess with the cutting edge of the pliers, to create a neat finish.

10 Once the straining wires have been attached to the corner posts and tightly stretched, attach them to the intermediate standards. Do this by winding the wire neatly, as in step 9, but with a smaller gauge binding wire than previously used.

11 When these wires are secure, attach the wire mesh. Start at a corner, attaching one end to the top of the post. Wrap the binding wire several times around the post and through the mesh, then twist the ends with the pliers to tighten and neaten.

12 Finally, working along the full length of the fence, pull the wire mesh taut, and attach it firmly to the straining wires at regular intervals on all levels. Do this by looping the thinner binding wire around the diamond mesh and the horizontal straining wires.

All types of brick are suitable for garden walls (see page 22), but facebrick is a particularly good choice as it looks attractive and is easy to maintain. The basic technique of laying bricks is quite easy to master, provided the basic principles of construction are followed (see pages 30–35).

Both half-brick (built with a single skin of brickwork) and one-brick (which comprises a double skin) walls may be built in the garden – the choice will depend on both the length and height of the structure you are planning. Local building regulations contain minimum specifications, but all longish walls must always be supported by piers or pillars, and they should have regular expansion joints (see page 50, step 12) every 6–7 m.

Even though this 5 m-long wall is only about 800 mm high, it consists of a double skin and includes two stocky pillars to accommodate an entrance.

MATERIALS
Brick sizes are reasonably standard worldwide and so it is quite easy to work out how many you will need. First estimate the area of the proposed wall; for every square metre of double wall (like the one featured here) you will need about 110 bricks, and about 55 for a single wall. Quantities for pillars will depend on whether two, three or four bricks are used for each course.

The ratio of cement and sand used for the bricklaying mortar will depend on the type of wall you are building. For freestanding garden walls built with clay brick, a 1:4 cement:sand mixture is often recommended; for a more workable mortar, add builders' lime in the ratio of 2:1 cement:lime. This will result in a 1:½:4 cement:lime:sand mix. You will need about 50 kg cement for every 200 bricks in a half-brick (single) wall and every 150 bricks in a one-brick (double) wall.

If the wall is to be rendered, use a similar 1:4 cement:sand mixture – 50 kg will be enough for about 1 m².

FOUNDATIONS
A solid foundation is a prerequisite for all walls. Dimensions, however, depend on the design of the wall as well as on soil conditions in your garden. Minimum specifications for a low half-brick wall stipulate a strip foundation at least 300 mm wide and 100 mm deep. The foundation for a thicker wall will be wider and deeper (see page 33 and below).

Note that if your wall is to be higher than the one illustrated here, the foundations must be more substantial.

BONDING
It is essential to bond brickwork so that the units are 'tied' together to form a solid mass, and to ensure that the load of the materials is evenly distributed along the length of the entire structure. To do this the bricks are laid so that the joints do not coincide with one another; at the same time they create a regular, and quite attractive, pattern.

There are several types of accepted bond patterns, some of which are more popular than others. The most common, which is particularly simple for the beginner builder to lay, is known as stretcher bond. This has bricks laid in consecutive courses overlapping one another by half. In a single wall, half bricks are laid at the ends to allow for bonding; in a double wall, the end bricks may be laid across the width of the wall, as headers.

Other options include the particularly strong English bond, English garden wall bond, American bond and Flemish bond, all of which involve laying both stretchers and headers and so are only suitable for one-brick walls.

1 Use pegs and line or string to mark out the area of the 300 mm-wide strip foundation. Remove the sods of grass and dig to the required depth, in this case about 110 mm. Mix the concrete (see page 34) and lay the foundation.

2 The foundation is always wider than the wall itself. When it has set (usually overnight), string a line along the length of the proposed structure to indicate the face of the wall and loose lay the first course of bricks, adjusting to avoid cutting.

3 Mark the position of the first few bricks and then mix mortar using the recommended ratio of cement and sand. Place a 'sausage' of mortar where the bricks are to be laid, flattening it slightly before bedding the first course in place.

4 If pillars or piers are to be incorporated, it is a good idea to loose lay bricks (as in step 2) to determine exactly where they will be built. An additional 600 mm x 600 mm foundation must be excavated and concreted for these structures.

5 Lay the courses of the pillar in the same way as the wall, taking care to ensure that all four corners are at right-angles. Once the bricks are in place, use a builder's square to check the angles. Correct any inaccuracies at this stage.

6 It is usually wise to reinforce brick pillars. Either insert a metal rod into the foundation or, if it is a low wall, into wet mortar poured into the central cavity of the pillar. You may need to support the metal with battens while you work.

7 Once you have started work on the pillars, continue to lay the wall and pillar courses consecutively. It is essential that all the brick courses are absolutely level. Remember to use a spirit level to check both vertical and horizontal planes regularly.

8 Also keep checking all internal and external corners with a builder's square. If you are planning to fit a light on one or other pillar, insert conduiting alongside the reinforcing rod. This way, wires may be inserted by an electrician later.

9 An efficient bricklayer will 'butter' the end of each brick he or she is laying, but there will still be some gaps between some of the bricks. These may be filled by slotting additional mortar into the joint. Use the trowel to tap it into place.

10 It always pays to work neatly, especially if you are using facebricks which will not be rendered with mortar or painted. As you lay the bricks, it is inevitable that some mortar will ooze out of the joints: scrape any excess off with the trowel.

11 The best way to ensure that all brick courses are equal is to use a gauge rod – a straight-edged piece of wood marked off to indicate one brick plus a 10 mm mortar joint. Once the wall is complete, rake out the joints with a pointing tool.

12 If you need to cut clay bricks, you can do so reasonably easily with the chisel end of a brick hammer (as shown), or with a bolster (or brickset) and a heavy club hammer. It is not usually necessary to use an angle grinder or other power tool.

Reconstituted (reconstructed) stone blocks have become a very popular substitute for difficult-to-obtain natural stone. Not only do they look remarkably like the real thing, but they are made in a wide range of sizes. The beauty of many reconstituted stone walls lies in the interesting bonding patterns created by using different-sized blocks. Moulded from concrete and tinted with coloured pigments, their regular (and uniform) shape makes them relatively easy to lay.

MATERIALS

Many people prefer to mix a number of different sizes of stone blocks for interest, rather than using just one size. Suppliers will provide random quantities based on the overall area of the wall. To work out your quantities, you need to know the dimensions of all block sizes to be incorporated, and then decide what proportion of each will be used. This wall uses blocks of the following heights and proportions: 75 mm (11%), 100 mm (35%), 125 mm (38%) and 150 mm (16%), and lengths vary from 200 mm to 325 mm. Jumper blocks are used randomly, comprising 12% of the surface.

Requirements for foundations and mortar are the same as those in the concrete block wall on page 48.

BONDING

Mix sizes throughout the wall to create attractive bonding patterns. The blocks may be laid in straight layers or with extended jumper blocks.

1 Start by marking out the foundation as shown on page 49 and excavate to the required depth. Hammer pegs into the ground to mark where the upper level of the concrete will come to. Then mix the concrete and place it in the trench.

2 Use a spade or trowel to tamp down the concrete. This will compact it and expel any air bubbles in the mixture. Smooth it out with the trowel or with a straight-edged piece of wood. Allow the mixture to set overnight before laying the blocks.

3 Use pegs to set up a builders' line which will accurately indicate the position of the front of the wall. Put a 'sausage' of mortar on the concrete and lay the first block against the line, using the handle of the trowel to knock it into place.

4 Continue with a bedding layer of mortar which should be about 100 mm wide and 10–12 mm thick. Flatten the mortar slightly with the trowel and then draw the trowel through the centre to make a slightly uneven furrow before laying blocks.

5 There are no rules to determine the order in which reconstituted stone blocks should be laid. By selecting a range of different sizes at random, you will create the effect of natural dressed stone wall. A jumper block is two or three courses high.

6 Lay all the blocks in the first course in position, leaving a gap of about 10 mm between blocks for the mortar joints. Then go back and fill all the spaces with mortar. It doesn't matter if the joints are slightly different widths – this will add authenticity.

7 Start the second course by spreading mortar on top of the first course. Bed each block in place, tamping it down to leave a joint 10 mm thick, and check that it is level. Use standard-height blocks next to the jumper blocks in the first course.

8 For a really good effect which will echo the solidity of stone, it is best to lay a double wall. Since different-sized blocks have been used for the wall, it is necessary to build the lower section to one height before constructing pillars.

9 Do not use too many different-sized blocks to build pillars. For ease of construction, use blocks of the same height for each course, choosing lengths that fit the dimensions of the structure. Use a trowel to scrape away excess mortar as you work.

10 Use your trowel to point or fill the joints between the blocks with mortar. Do not worry if any of the excess mortar falls into the central cavity; it is preferable to have a solid pillar, rather than one that is hollow in the middle (see step 13).

11 Even though reconstituted stone blocks are relatively irregular in shape and uneven in finish, it is essential to use a spirit level from time to time to check that both horizontal and vertical planes are straight and level (see page 31).

12 Use a piece of cut metal or a pointing trowel to scrape out the mortar joints neatly. As the two skins of this wall are laid about 60 mm apart, some of the joints in the sides of the pillars will be considerably thicker than those in the wall.

13 Before adding the capping, fill the gap between the two skins of the wall with mortar. Tamp it down well, then place a thick layer of mortar on top of the wall and level it out with a length of wood or the edge of your spirit level.

14 Reconstituted stone paving slabs are an ideal choice for the capping, since they match the colour and finish of the wall blocks. Place them on the mortar bed so they overhang the wall face slightly. Leave a 10 mm joint between the slabs.

15 Check the upper surface of the paving blocks with a spirit level and use a rubber mallet to gently tap any blocks which may be out of alignment. Use the trowel to fill the gaps between the pavers with mortar. Clean any excess from the surface.

Walls built from ordinary concrete blocks are sturdy, generally inexpensive and relatively quick to build since the units are larger than regular bricks, and usually hollow. They are available all over the world in a wide variety of sizes, and are used for many types of construction. Most freestanding garden walls are built with only one thickness of block; if added strength is required, these structures are simply reinforced (see below).

Although ordinary concrete building blocks are not particularly appealing on their own, they are an ideal material for garden walls. Furthermore, given a mortar rendering and a coat of paint, they can look very attractive indeed.

MATERIALS
The blocks used for this wall measure 390 mm x 190 mm x 190 mm and, like most concrete blocks, they are hollow. To build 8 m² of wall you will need 100 blocks of this size (12½ blocks per 1 m²). If larger blocks are used, it stands to reason that fewer blocks will be required.

If your blocks are a different size, calculate the surface area of your proposed wall and simply divide this by the area of one block (height x length). To avoid excessive cutting, it is best to base the overall dimensions of the wall on the blocks you plan to use.

The mortar mix used to lay the blocks will determine how much cement, sand and, possibly, lime will be required. Generally, a weaker mix is used for concrete blocks than for bricks and a ratio of 1:6 cement to sand is a common option. To lay 1 000 concrete blocks measuring 390 mm x 190 mm x 190 mm, you need 325 kg cement, 162.5 kg lime (if required) and 1.3 m³ sand.

The mortar rendering should be compatible with the mortar used to lay the blocks. If a 1:6 mixture is used, you can cover an area of 7 m² with 50 kg cement and 300 kg sand.

Cement, crushed stone (aggregate) and suitable sand will also be required for the foundations.

FEATURES
Various features may be incorporated into a block wall, including planters, a door or gate, an arch, letterbox and even a compartment to store rubbish bins out of sight. This wall includes an arched door, corner planter and, on the inside, a low seat and a rubbish bin compartment. It is essential to plan for these features, as you will have to dig additional foundations to accommodate them in terms of your design.

The planter is formed by building the wall across one of the corners and then continuing the straight lines of the structure two courses above ground level. The bin compartment is made by building a 600 mm-high wall to create three sides of a 600 mm x 600 mm box which sits at 90° to the boundary wall. You need formwork to create an opening on the boundary (see page 50, step 10); this can be fitted with a simple wooden door.

FOUNDATIONS
Solid concrete foundations are essential for all concrete block walls. The depth must support the mass of the structure and so is determined primarily by the height and width of the wall to be built. If hardcore is to be included under the concrete, you will have to further increase the depth of the trench to accommodate it. Remember that the foundation must be wider than the wall (see page 33).

Although the foundation for this block wall is 200 mm deep, the trench itself is about 300 mm deep, so that the first course is partially below ground.

REINFORCING
Very high concrete block walls, or those that are to retain soil, should be reinforced. Foundation reinforcing will usually be specified by an engineer,

but there is no reason why you should not set it in place yourself. It involves laying a grid of steel in the trench before the concrete is poured, and does not require any special skills.

Vertical reinforcing may also be necessary, but since concrete blocks have a hollow core, this is simple to accommodate. Steel bars are set in the concrete foundation (as indicated in steps 3 and 7 on page 49) and the hollow core of the blocks placed over them during the laying process.

Another type of reinforcing which may be required involves laying a wire grid of brickforce, supplied in a roll, over the horizontal plane of some courses (usually every four or five courses). It is not necessary to lay it on every course and may, in fact, only be incorporated over openings left in the wall for doors or other features.

BONDING
Laying concrete blocks is very similar to bricklaying, only you may find that blocks are more cumbersome to work with. Just as brick courses must bond with one another, so too must the courses in a concrete block wall. Since the finished surface of a standard block wall will invariably be rendered, they are laid in a stretcher bond (rather than any other patterned bond), with each block overlapping the one below it by half a block.

Although screen (pierced) blocks are laid in the same way as ordinary concrete blocks, they can't be vertically reinforced and so a straightforward stack bond is normally used. This is why a screen block wall should always include pillars for extra strength.

CUTTING BLOCKS
It is not easy to cut blocks accurately with a brickhammer, although an uneven edge will not usually create problems if you are to render the surface. Use an angle grinder to produce a clean cut.

1 Set out the foundations accurately: hammer in pegs and then string a taut line between them. The dimensions of the foundations will depend on the design of the wall (including any features) and the size of the concrete blocks being used.

2 It is helpful to mark the area to be excavated with chalk, cement or flour so that the pegs can be removed before you dig the foundation trenches. The depth of the excavation will depend on the height and thickness of your wall.

3 Reinforcing may be required for some garden walls, especially if they are relatively high. Check that the foundation floor is flat and level, before placing any reinforcing specified in the design. Wire the rods together to form a stable framework.

4 You will need to indicate the proposed position of the upper surface of the concrete foundations: knock metal or wooden pegs firmly into the ground at various intervals, allowing them to protrude to the required height, in this case 200 mm.

5 Mix the concrete by hand or in a motorised concrete mixer (see page 34). For large jobs, it is worth ordering ready-mix concrete to be delivered to the site in special trucks. Spread it out evenly in the foundation trench to the height of the pegs.

6 Build up the wall course by course in stretcher bond, checking regularly that the blocks are level and that all corners are truly square. Here a section of brickwork from the original patio is incorporated at the base of the wall.

7 If reinforcing rods are being used, centre the blocks over them and fill in the cavities with mortar. For extra strength, you can also incorporate brickforce in the mortar bed (see step 11). Use a builder's square to check the outside corner.

8 As you work, fill in the holes in the blocks with mortar to create a solid structure. Continue to lay the blocks in a stretcher bond pattern, so that each one overlaps the block in the course below by half. Check regularly with the spirit level.

9 Any special features should be built into the wall as construction progresses. For a low seat, lay an additional course of blocks on the inside of the wall and top with terrace blocks laid on their sides; or lay two block courses and screed the surface.

10 For a rubbish bin compartment formwork is set in place to support the opening while building continues. Once the mortar is dry, the formwork is removed. Once the wall has been plastered, a door may be fitted to conceal the bin from sight.

11 In addition to foundation and vertical reinforcing, wire (brickforce) may be laid between some of the block courses to further strengthen the wall and minimise the risk of cracking. This is especially important over the opening for the bin.

12 It is essential to provide expansion joints every 6–7 metres to allow natural horizontal movement in the wall. Since these joints must extend the full height of the wall, blocks will have to be cut and half blocks used every second course.

13 If lighting or a security system is to be incorporated into the wall, conduiting must be put in place during construction. You can do this yourself, but it is essential to ask an electrician to advise on the correct connections and to install the wiring.

14 If you want to include a door opening in the wall, build the frame into the blockwork as the wall rises. Use a braced prop to keep it vertical. Here its sill rests on a soldier course of bricks to form a neat step up to the higher level beyond the wall.

15 When the blockwork is complete and the mortar has set, mix cement and sand in the same ratio used for blocklaying (see page 48), adding lime if you wish. Put some of the mixture on a mortar board. Then use a plasterer's trowel to lay it on.

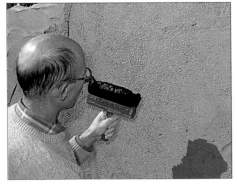

16 Cover the surface fairly roughly not forgetting the tops of the wall and bin box, applying pressure with the trowel to ensure the mortar sticks. Leave to set for about an hour. Then use a straight-edge to carefully scrape and smooth any excess mortar.

17 The finished rendering should now be 10–15 mm thick. Once you have scraped the wall, you can float the surface to smooth it out further. First splash a little water onto the surface with a wet paintbrush, working in fairly small areas at a time.

18 Use a wooden float to smooth the moistened surface. If you wish, you can use a steel float to get an even more uniform finish, but this is not normally necessary for a garden wall. Do not over-trowel, as this may cause surface cracks.

The simplest way to build a retaining wall is to use concrete modular blocks which interlock with one another to create a stable structure. These are manufactured in several shapes and sizes, from relatively lightweight, rectangular terrace blocks (see page 53) to much heavier units, most of which are plantable. Although there are obvious differences in the various designs, foundations, drainage requirements and basic method of construction remain the same. Mortar is not generally necessary unless extra reinforcing is specified by an engineer (see page 23).

The 200 mm-high blocks used here are shaped so that the convex curve of one block fits into the concave curve of the next. The rounded edge or the flat face may be used for the outer face. By simply turning the units very slightly it is possible to create a curved wall. This wall is 1.2 m high, and is stepped back gradually to create a plantable surface. It includes a seat, an open planter, and a totally vertical section. Steps can be included if the wall is to create a terrace.

FOUNDATION

The foundation must be properly prepared and level. Most low walls may be built on well-compacted earth or gravel, but a wall higher than 1.5 m or one built on poor ground needs a concrete foundation (see page 32). The top of the finished foundation should be at least 150 mm below ground level.

1 Decide on the design of your wall and then peg it out to show where the foundation trench will be located. Both the height of the wall and the angle at which the units are to be stepped back will determine the width of the foundation.

2 String a line along the length of the proposed wall, to indicate the location of the back of the finished structure. This is especially important if it is a boundary wall which must be accurately positioned. Then excavate a trench about 600 mm wide.

3 String a second line to show where the wall will start and then compact the soil with a punner. If a concrete foundation is required, remember that the trench will have to be at least 200 mm deeper to accommodate this material.

4 Use a spirit level to check that all foundations are absolutely level. If the ground slopes, you will usually be able to step the foundation by the height of one unit. This means you will need an extra course of blocks on the lower level.

5 Position the first block and make sure it is level. When building on a concrete foundation, use a small amount of mortar under each block of the bottom row to facilitate accurate levelling and to help lock the blocks in place.

6 Use pegs and a builder's line to ensure that the front of the wall is straight. If you are battling to get the first course level, put a little soil into each block and then manoeuvre them slightly so that the extra earth fills in gaps under the blocks.

7 Regularly check on levels and alignment, using a club hammer or rubber mallet to gently knock the blocks straight. If the first course is not laid correctly, and the blocks are not level, the rest of the wall will be thrown out of alignment.

8 Fill the blocks with top soil and backfill behind the blocks as each row is completed. Backfill material will depend on the design and height of the wall and the site. It is best to use a layer of free-draining river sand, especially at the base of the wall.

9 Most modular blocks are commonly laid in a stretcher bond pattern, although a stack bond may also be suitable, for instance if the wall is to be vertical. Where cutting is necessary, it is best to use an angle grinder or brick hammer.

10 This two-course high section of vertical wall has been designed to create a seating area. A backfill layer of crushed stone is incorporated for drainage and the second course of blocks backfilled with stone. This can be screeded with mortar if you wish.

11 Use soil to fill in over the crushed stone backfill and compact as before, using a punner or ramming tool. Note that it may be necessary to include a much deeper layer of coarse stone or sand. Consult an engineer if necessary.

12 The third course of blocks, which is laid above the surface of the seat, only just overlaps the second course, thus ensuring maximum width. The flat face of the unit is reversed to face outwards to create a comfortable backrest.

13 At the end of the seat, the blocks are reversed again and positioned to create a planter box. This entails compacting a shelf behind the blocks which have already been laid. It should be level with the upper surface of these blocks.

14 Continue to dry stack the blocks, stepping back and positioning according to your design plan. As each course progresses, it is helpful to place a row of blocks on their sides nearby so that you do not have to fetch individual units.

15 Concrete blocks at the ends of a retaining wall may be feathered out or curved inwards. Make certain all blocks are filled with top soil and the area directly behind the wall is backfilled and compacted. Watering the backfill will aid compaction.

Considerably smaller and lighter than the sturdy, rounded blocks used for the retaining wall on pages 51–52, these concrete terrace blocks are perfect for retaining soil within the garden itself. Various types are available, ranging from units which give an open checkerboard appearance to those with a closed vertical surface. All interlink or interlock for strength and stability. Like the larger retaining blocks, terrace blocks are generally plantable, which means you can cover the concrete structure with creepers, climbers or even small shrubs in a relatively short space of time.

The blocks used here measure 400 mm x 200 mm x 200 mm and are basically rectangular in shape. This particular design features a convex corner diagonally opposite a concave corner (to interlock with an adjoining block) and a right-angled corner diagonally opposite one that is cut out to form a matching

angle (also for secure interlocking). Although they can be laid in various ways they are placed diagonally for this step-by-step sequence. Any similar block could be used in the same way, but since designs do vary, be sure to follow any special instructions offered by the particular manufacturer.

The wall featured here was laid beneath a timber deck to stabilise a sloping bank. Although the angle was not particularly steep, soil was frequently washed away in rainy weather. The wall is only a metre high and simple for an amateur to tackle.

While there are no special features incorporated here, the blocks could be laid on their sides to form either a seat (see step 9 on page 49) or to create a flight of steps leading to the top terrace. Note that if feature elements (like steps and seats) are included in your design, it is essential to fill the blocks with either a weak mortar mix or sand.

FOUNDATION

Although it is not necessary to throw a concrete foundation for a retaining wall of this height and constructed by this method, it is vital that the earth beneath the wall is stable and well compacted. If the soil is soft, it is essential to dig a foundation trench and to fill it with gravel or very fine (9.5 or 10 mm) crushed stone, which should also be compacted with a punner or ramming tool.

BACKFILL

In most instances, you can use the excavated soil to backfill a low terrace wall. If you have removed clay, however, you will need to bring in additional building sand, which allows the water to drain more freely. In this case, it would also be wise to backfill the first course or two with crushed stone or gravel to further aid drainage. Good quality soil must be used to fill blocks which will be planted.

1 Mark out the position of the terrace block wall and dig a trench about 200 mm deep and 600 mm wide. Compact well with a punner. Use a spirit level to check that the surface is flat.

2 Set up a line along the front of the trench by tying string around blocks at either end. Lay the blocks so that they interlock firmly for stability and the rounded corner is flush with the line.

3 Make sure that the blocks are level and fill behind them with gravel, sand or the excavated soil. If you plan to plant the wall, be sure to fill the blocks with good quality soil

4 The second row of blocks is laid over the first, but stepped back slightly to create pockets for planting. Use a spirit level regularly to ensure that the horizontal plane is level.

5 You will need to lay five courses for a 1 m-high wall. Backfill each course and all the blocks as you work. It is also best to compact the sand or soil behind the wall as it progresses.

6 There must be no voids behind the wall or in the blocks themselves. A good way to ensure that the soil is properly compacted is to hose the wall once it is complete.

This remarkably simple construction creates an attractive basketweave effect between timber poles. The ends of relatively thin horizontal slats, positioned close together, are nailed alternately to the front and the back of each pole. Left to weather naturally, the fence will soon develop a lovely rustic appeal. The materials listed are sufficient for one 2.3 m x 2.2 m panel, and presume you will be using a 1:4:4 concrete mix. Additional adjacent panels will, of course, require only one extra pole each.

MATERIALS

Footings for 2 poles
60 kg cement
245 kg sand
245 kg stone
hardcore and/or soil for fill

Fasteners
88 x 100 mm anodised
  wire nails

Fencing
2 x 3 m poles, 120 mm
  in diameter
22 x 2.2 m x 95 mm x
  15 mm slats (or similar)

1 Mark the position of the fence and peg out the footings at 1.98 m centres.
2 Dig 750 mm-deep footings, 750 mm x 750 mm in size.
3 Brace the poles in position and check that they are vertical.
4 Mix the concrete as described on page 34.
5 Pack the footings about two-thirds full with concrete. When the concrete has set, add enough soil to fill the holes completely. Alternatively, first put a 200 mm-deep layer of hardcore into each hole and then top up with concrete. Leave to set.
6 Before removing the bracing, nail the slats to the poles, alternately bringing one slat to the front of the pole, and then one to the back. Start from the bottom and use two nails at each end of the slats.

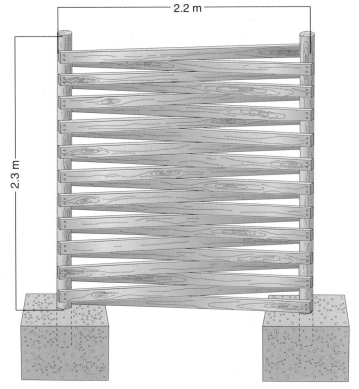

This attractive patio screen, made as shown in the step-by-step instructions on page 37, has been mounted on a low wall to shield the seating area from the neighbouring house. The screen is made by attaching 30 mm x 12 mm laths to a framework which is bolted to the wall and nailed to two supporting poles. Although the screen shown in the photograph is attached to the pergola beams, the plan allows for a freestanding screen. Materials for the 1.3 m-high wall are not included.

MATERIALS

Footings
50 kg cement
200 kg sand
200 kg stone

Panels
2 x 4 m machined poles,
  90 mm in diameter
2 x 4.25 m x 50 mm x
  32 mm lengths timber
  (or 2 shorter lengths
  joined with a lap joint)
1 x 2.3 m x 72 mm x 32 mm
  length timber

48 x 2 m x 30 mm x
  12 mm horizontal laths
52 x 1.8 m x 30 mm x
  12 mm vertical laths

Fasteners
2 x 100 mm masonry
  anchor bolts
2 x No. 8 (4.2 mm) x 50 mm
  brass screws
200 x 40 mm anodised
  wire nails
4 x 75 mm anodised
  wire nails
panel pins (optional)

1 Mark out 500 mm x 500 mm footings for the two poles at 4.16 m centres, and dig to a depth of 500 mm.

2 Position the poles in the footings and brace, making sure they are vertical.

3 Mix concrete in a cement:sand:stone ratio of 1:4:4 and pour into the holes. Allow the concrete to set.

4 Nail the 4.25 m lengths of timber to the top of the poles and 1.7 m down from the top respectively.

5 Position the 2.3 m-long central timber, allowing the overlap to extend at the bottom. Bolt it to the low wall, and screw to the framework.

6 Nail the horizontal laths into position, ensuring they are equally spaced.

7 Then nail the vertical laths into place, using panel pins at the joints for added stability if required.

8 Finish the screen with the paint or sealant of your choice.

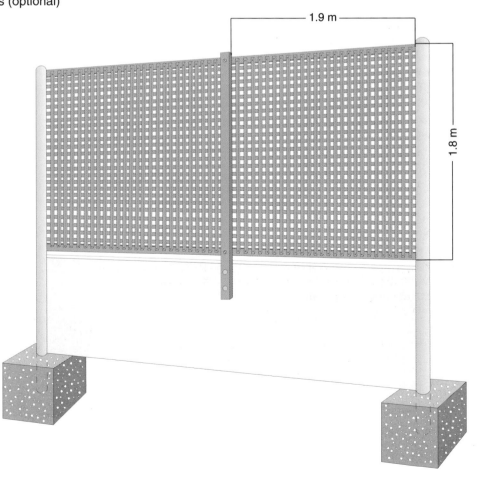

A plain picket fence and matching gate have been painted bright blue to add character and impact. Attached to stocky pillars, the 2.75 m-wide gateway is perfect for a driveway. (A single gate would be more useful in the garden.) The materials list will enable you to build the gate and pillars. You can make adjacent panels with 20 pickets attached to 2.1 m x 38 mm x 38 mm battens; attach these to 90 mm-diameter poles or planed timber posts as shown on pages 38–41.

MATERIALS

Foundations
100 kg cement
405 kg sand
405 kg stone

Pillars
264 bricks
100 kg cement
50 kg lime (optional)
395 kg sand
2 x 1.5 m reinforcing rods

Gate
2 x 1.05 m x 38 mm x
  38 mm battens

4 x 1.33 x 90 mm x 35 mm
  bracing timbers
2 x 1.5 x 90 mm x 35 mm
  bracing timbers
26 x 1.2 m x 70 mm x
  20 mm pickets, with
  tops cut to a point

Fasteners
4 x No 10 (4.9 mm) x 100 mm
  masonry anchor bolts
156 x No 6 (3.5 mm) x
  32 mm brass screws
4 x barrel hinges with
  screws
latch and screws

1 Peg out the position of the two pillars at 4 m centres.
2 Mark out the area for the two 900 mm x 900 mm foundation footings.
3 Dig the footings to a depth of 250 mm. Mix concrete in a 1:4:4 ratio of cement:sand:stone. Pour the concrete into the holes, compact, level and leave to set thoroughly.
4 Build the two pillars, alternating courses as shown in the illustration. Fill the central cavity with mortar as you work.

5 When you have laid about three courses, insert a reinforcing rod into the still-wet mortar of each pillar. The rods will extend to the top of each pillar. Brace with timber to stop them falling to one side.
6 When you have laid about 20 courses (more if the foundation was slightly below ground level), lay a slightly wider course of bricks to create a lip.
7 Form the capping by building each of the next three courses progressively smaller in dimension, to form a pyramid shape as shown in the illustration.
8 When the mortar has set, mix additional batches to render the surface, and fill in the gaps in the capping.
9 Allow the rendered mortar to dry thoroughly, then attach the battens to the inside surface of each pillar. Use two masonry anchor bolts on each side.
10 Now assemble the first half of the gate. Lay the two horizontal, 1.33 m lengths of the Z-brace 800 mm apart on a flat work surface and screw a picket to each end at 90°.
11 The diagonal, 1.5 m length of bracing must be cut at an angle at each end. Place it diagonally across the middle to form a Z and mark a cutting edge. Saw the ends neatly.
12 Slot the bracing in place. Drill through the bracing into the picket at the points where the pieces of wood meet, then screw in place.
13 Now position and secure the rest of the pickets in the same way, using a 35 mm spacer to ensure the gaps between them are even, and carefully lining up the base of each picket so that the bottom of the gate will be level.
14 Attach the gate to the battens with roll hinges, and fit the latch.
15 Repeat steps 10–14 for the other half of the gate.
16 Finish with the paint and/or sealant of your choice.

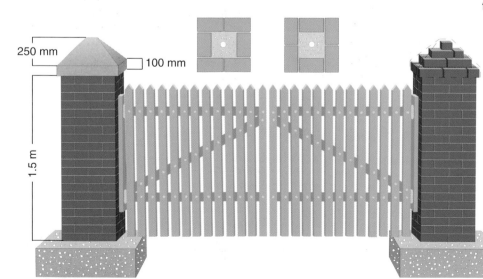

250 mm

100 mm

1.5 m

Attractive panels, made by attaching timber slats on the diagonal, are set between recessed, precast concrete posts, to create a good-looking fence which offers privacy and security. A narrow, precast concrete panel is slotted horizontally into place at the base of the timber panels. If precast materials are not available, this design may be adapted for timber posts or masonry pillars. In this case, build a low wall in place of the base panel or position the timber closer to the ground. While the illustration shows two adjacent panels, the materials are sufficient for one panel between two posts.

MATERIALS
Foundations
100 kg cement
405 kg sand
405 kg stone

Framework
2 x 2.35 m x 130 mm x
   120 mm precast concrete
   posts, with 50 mm
   recesses in both sides
1 x 1.28 m x 200 mm x
   45 mm precast concrete
   panel

Panel
2 x 1.48 m x 70 mm x
   20 mm lengths timber
3 x 1.17 m x 70 mm x
   20 mm lengths timber
24 x 70 mm x 15 mm slats
   to fit 2 m², cut to lengths
   from 300 mm to 1.95 m

Fasteners
144 x 25 mm anodised
   wire nails
6 x 100 mm anodised
   wire nails

1 Mark the positon of the proposed fence and peg out the footings at about 1.4 m centres.
2 Mark the 600 mm x 600 mm footings with chalk or flour.
3 Dig the footings to a depth of 600 mm.
4 Brace the posts in position with battens, making certain they are vertical, acccurately spaced and in a straight line. Concrete into position using a 1:4:4 mix.

5 Before the concrete sets, slide the base panel into position to ensure the posts are accurately spaced.
6 Check that the concrete is well compacted and leave to set overnight.
7 Working on a flat surface, position the five pieces of timber which will form the framework for each panel, placing the shorter lengths on the inside of the long pieces of timber.
8 Predrill three pilot holes in each 1.48 m-long piece of timber at the point where the shorter lengths are joined to it at right angles.
9 Join the framework together using the 100 mm-long nails.
10 Position one of the slats diagonally across the centre of the panel, and mark the cutting lines at the correct angles. Trim with a tenon saw.
11 Continue to mark and cut all the slats, ending with the shorter lengths.
12 Position the 24 slats across the framework, ensuring the gaps between them are even.
13 Nail the slats to the framework, using 25 mm-long nails at the top, bottom and middle, if necessary, of each slat.
14 Finally, slide the panel into the recesses in the posts (see illustration). If timber posts are used, nail or screw the panel into place. If you have built masonry pillars, bolt the framework to these before affixing the slats.

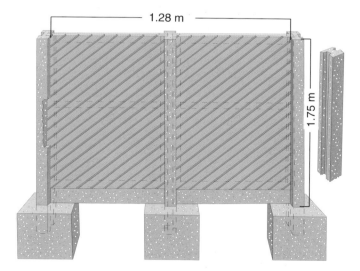

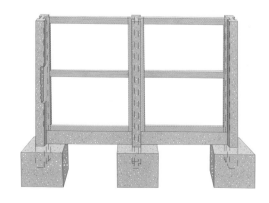

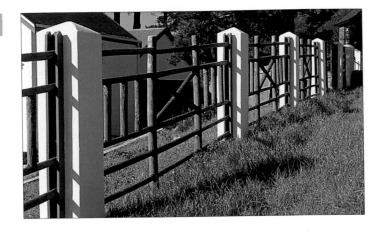

Machined poles are used ingeniously to create attractive fencing between rendered brick pillars. Holes are bored into the main uprights to accommodate the horizontal timbers, whilst the ends of the vertical poles are cut out in a slight V so that they can slot neatly into place. Planed pickets are affixed to the pillars to house the ends of the poles. The materials list specifies one approximately 4 m-long section of the fence only. It is not essential to use materials of identical dimensions; adjust the measurements on the plan to accommodate what is available.

MATERIALS

Foundation footings
115 kg cement
465 kg sand
465 kg stone

Pillars
200 bricks
75 kg cement
38 kg lime (optional)
300 kg sand

Fencing
6 x 1.6 m x 70 mm x 20 mm
  pickets
2 x 2.1 m upright poles,
  90 mm in diameter
10 x 1.65 m poles, 60 mm
  in diameter

2 x 1.12 m poles, 60 mm
  in diameter
5 x 1.08 m poles, 60 mm
  in diameter
6 x 500 mm poles, 60 mm
  in diameter

Fasteners
6 x No 8 (4.9 mm) x 75 mm
  coach screws with
  Rawl plugs or masonry
  anchor bolts
12 x No 6 (3.5 mm) x 50 mm
  countersunk screws
10 x 75 mm anodised
  wire nails
4 x 100 mm anodised
  wire nails

1 Set out the fence and mark out the position of all foundation footings.
2 Dig 500 mm x 500 mm x 500 mm footings for the poles, and 750 mm x 750 mm x 200 mm footings for the pillars.
3 Bore five shallow holes on either side of the upright posts as indicated in the illustration, using a router or wood chisel. Make sure that all the holes are accurately spaced to ensure that the horizontal poles will be parallel once slotted into position.

4 Brace the upright poles in position, using a spirit level to ensure that they are vertical, and check that the shallow holes are lined up correctly.
5 Mix concrete in a cement:sand:stone ratio of 1:4:4 and pour into all four footings. Make sure the concrete is well compacted and that tops of the pillar foundations are level.
6 Although the foundation for the pillars should set overnight, assemble the central panel of the fence while the concrete is still workable.
7 Starting from the bottom, slot the 1.08 m poles into place.
8 Cut curved blocks from the centre of each 1.12 m-long pole to enable you to create a lap joint.
9 Trim the ends of these crosspieces to fit the join between the vertical and horizontal posts, then slot into place and nail to the horizontal poles with the 100 mm-long nails.
10 Ensure the bracing is secure and that the upright poles are still vertical. Also ensure the concrete is well compacted.
11 When the remaining foundations have set, build the two brick pillars to a height of 1.6 m.
12 Once the mortar has set, mix another batch and render the pillars, creating a pointed capping if desired. Allow to set thoroughly before assembling the rest of the fence.
13 Use coach screws or masonry bolts to fix a picket to the inside surface of each pillar, ensuring they are centred.
14 Then position the remaining pickets at right angles to these, to form a casing to accommodate the end of the adjacent horizontal poles (see illustration). Fix these to the inside picket, using countersunk screws.
15 Slide the lower three 1.65 m horizontal poles into place on either side, nailing to picket casing.
16 Cut the ends of the 500 mm-long vertical poles to form a shallow V to enable you to brace them against the horizontal poles.
17 Evenly position three vertical poles on each side. Slide the next horizontal pole into position over the top of them.
18 Nail the last horizontal poles into place.
19 Finish with the sealant and/or paint of your choice.

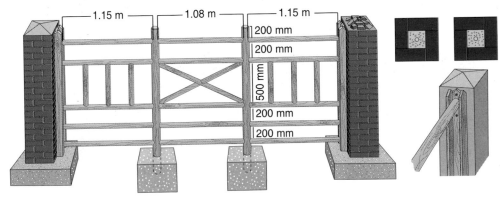

Lattice screen panels, made with thin, diagonal laths, have been mounted onto a low block wall between imposing pillars. The structure is angled at each end to give a curved effect. Precast concrete orbs fixed to the top of the pillars complete the design. The blocks may be rendered in the usual way, or simply smeared with mortar to give a lightly bagged finish. If the specified block sizes are not available in your area, adapt the plan and change the dimensions slightly. Materials are specified for one lattice panel only.

MATERIALS
Foundation
160 kg cement
650 kg (0.5 m³) sand
650 kg stone

Wall and pillars
330 x 290 mm x 90 mm x
   90 mm concrete blocks
96 x 190 mm x 90 mm x
   90 mm concrete blocks
300 kg cement
150 kg lime (optional)
0.9 m³ sand
5 x precast concrete orbs on
   300 mm x 300 mm base

Lattice panel
4 x 1.2 m x 50 mm x 30 mm
   lengths timber
1 x 1.2 m x 70 mm x 30 mm
   cover strip
80 m x 45 mm x 10 mm
   laths, cut to length to
   fit frame

Fasteners
4 x 100 mm anodised
   wire nails
110 x 25 mm anodised
   wire nails
8 x 75 mm masonry
   anchor bolts

1 Mark out the position of the structure, allowing for a 500 mm wide foundation.
2 Dig the foundation trench to a depth of 200 mm.
3 Mix concrete in a cement:sand:stone ratio of 1:4:4 and place it in the trench. Level and compact as described on page 34.
4 When the concrete has set, mark the position of the five pillars at 1.52 m centres.
5 Build up the pillars and wall sections, laying the blocks for the pillars and walls consecutively.

6 Lay an orb on top of each pillar, using a little of the mortar.
7 When the mortar has set, render the surface.
8 Position the framework for the lattice panel with the upright lengths on the inside. Use corner clamps to hold the timber at right angles and then nail the frame together with the 100 mm wire nails.
9 Cut the laths as you work, starting with the longest ones (about 1.8 m). As the laths are attached diagonally, cut each end at an angle to fit the frame.
10 Position the laths against the frame, allowing a gap of about 45 mm between each. Nail them to the frame, using the 25 mm wire nails.
11 Bolt the frame to the pillars, with the frame facing outwards.
12 Nail the cover strip to the top of the frame.
13 Finish with the sealant and/or paint of your choice.

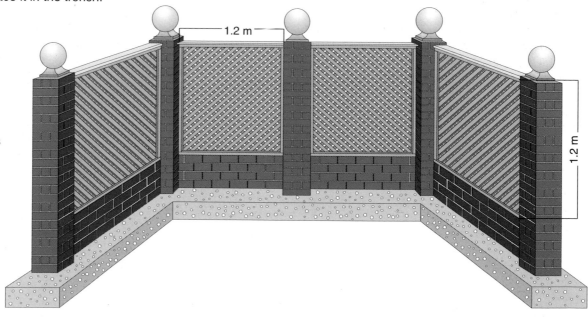

1.2 m

1.2 m

Rustic timber panels combine beautifully with natural stone pillars. If natural stone is not available in your area, use reconstituted stone blocks. These 2 m-high pillars are 700 mm x 700 mm in size, and the low 10 m-long wall which supports the fencing is 500 mm x 500 mm. If reconstituted stone blocks are used, proportions may be smaller. The slats are cut from rustic timber with bark still attached; any sawn timber may be used.

MATERIALS
Foundations
570 kg cement
1.7 m³ sand
1.7 m³ stone

Wall
stones for 4.5 m³
mortar (amount will depend
 on size of stones used)

Fencing
4 x 1.6 m upright poles,
90 mm in diameter
3 x 3.2 m x 75 mm x 50 mm
 support beams
2 x 450 mm x 75 mm x
 50 mm support beams
105 x 1.4 m x 95 mm x
 22 mm slats

Fasteners
8 x 100 mm anodised
 wire nails
210 x 50 mm anodised
 wire nails

1 Set out the foundations, allowing a width of 750 mm for the wall and 1 m for the pillars.
2 Dig a 250 mm-deep trench for the foundations.
3 Mix the concrete in the ratio 1:4:4 and place in the trench.
4 Compact, level and allow to set overnight.
5 Build the pillars and the wall, allowing slightly larger stones to overlap the top of each pillar and so form a natural capping.
6 Set the upright poles vertically in the stonework to a depth of 500 mm, as indicated, to provide a support for the timber.
7 Use a spirit level to ensure the poles are vertical, and brace them in position while the mortar dries.
8 Use the longer nails to fix the horizontal supporting timbers to the upright poles.
9 Then nail the slats to these beams.

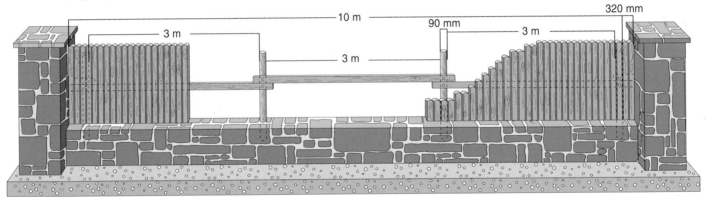

Clay screen (breeze) blocks have been attractively combined with facebrick pillars and a low, supporting one-brick wall along the boundary. Both the wall and top course of blocks, which is laid in the traditional stack bond, have been topped with a facebrick capping to create the effect of panels. This design is suitable for both flat and slightly sloping properties. Materials specified will enable you to build two pillars and an approximately 1.6 m-long section of pierced block wall, using facebricks and 150 mm x 150 mm x 110 mm blocks. If blocks in your area are a different size, simply adjust the overall measurement of the wall to fit.

MATERIALS
Foundations
65 kg cement
265 kg sand
265 kg stone

Wall
242 facebricks
60 x 150 mm x 150 mm x
 110 mm screen blocks
155 kg cement
630 kg sand
brickforce (reinforcing)

1 Mark out the foundations, ensuring they are about 500 mm wide. The pillars will be at about 2 m centres.
2 Dig the foundation trench to a depth of 250 mm, stepping it down at each pillar if the ground slopes.
3 Mix the concrete in the ratio 1:4:4 and place in the trench, compacting and levelling in the usual way.
4 When the concrete has set, start laying the bricks.
5 Mix the mortar in a cement:sand ratio of 1:4, adding 25 kg lime to each 50 kg cement if you wish.
6 Lay three courses in a stretcher bond.
7 Top the section of wall between the two pillars with bricks laid on-edge to form a header course.
8 Start building up the pillars as shown. Place reinforcing over every third course.

9 Lay the screen blocks in a stack bond, positioning them along the central line of the supporting wall.
10 Finish off by laying bricks on-edge along the top of the entire wall, including pillars. Since the blocks are not as wide as the supporting wall, neaten the base of the block portion with a little extra mortar if you wish.

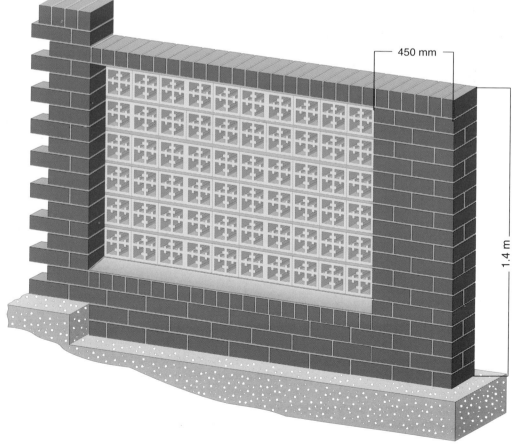

450 mm

1.4 m

Here a series of short walls laid at 90° to one another create a zigzag effect. To add interest, every second section of the wall is built slightly higher than the previous one. Constructed to screen the front entrance of a suburban house from the road, the wall is built with ordinary bricks in a stretcher bond and is then rendered and painted in the usual way. A flower bed in front of the wall adds colour and interest.

MATERIALS
Foundations
425 kg cement
1.3 m³ sand
1.3 m³ stone

Bricklaying
2 250 bricks
560 kg cement
260 kg lime (optional)
1.6 m³ sand
brickforce (reinforcing)

Mortar for rendering
260 kg cement
130 kg lime
0.8 m³ sand

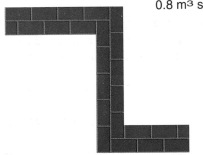

1 Peg out the wall foundation as shown on the plan, ensuring it is about 750 mm wide.
2 Dig out the trench to a depth of 250 mm.
3 Mix the concrete in a cement:sand:stone ratio of 1:4:4 and place in the trench, compacting well, and levelling with a straight-edged piece of wood.
4 When the concrete is well set, start laying the bricks in a stretcher bond. Leave a slight gap between the two skins of brickwork and lay reinforcing on top of every third course.
5 Step every second section of the wall up two courses, as indicated, so that the lowest section is 2 m (25 courses) above ground level, and the highest is 2.6 m (31 courses).
6 Allow the mortar to set, before rendering the surface as illustrated on page 50.

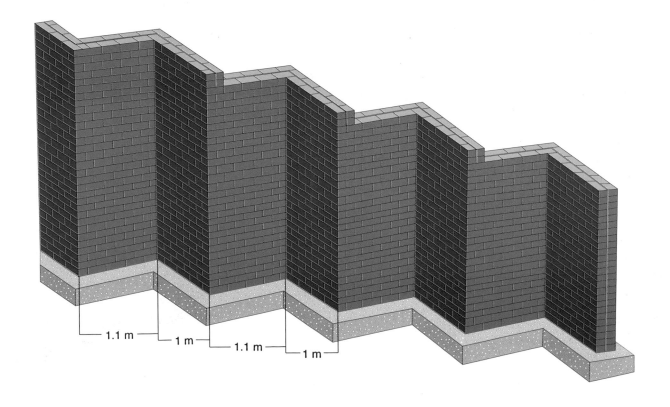

1.1 m — 1 m — 1.1 m — 1 m

A sturdy boundary wall built with concrete blocks incorporates planters in alternate sections of the structure. The wall is constructed between attractive pillars, and the sections which back the planters are stepped back by 700 mm. As this design is imposing in effect, it is particularly well suited to a large property, but could be adapted for just about any location. Materials specified are sufficient for a 6.5 m-long section of wall, as illustrated in the plan.

MATERIALS
Foundations
365 kg cement
1.6 m³ sand
1.6 m³ stone

Blockwork
185 x 390 mm x 190 mm x
  190 mm concrete blocks
60 kg cement
30 kg lime (optional)

365 kg (0.3 m³) sand
brickforce (optional)

Mortar for rendering
150 kg cement
75 kg lime
0.7 m³ sand

1 Mark out the position of the wall as illustrated, with pillars at 3 m centres. Make sure the stepped-back sections are at right-angles to the pillars.
2 Mark the area of the foundations, allowing a width of 500 mm for the wall sections and 1 m x 1 m for the pillars.
3 Dig the foundation trenches to a depth of at least 250 mm.
4 Mix the concrete in a cement:sand:stone ratio of 1:4:4 and place it in the prepared trench. Ensure it is well compacted and level. Leave to set overnight.
5 Mix the mortar in a cement:sand ratio of 1:6, adding the lime if required.
6 Build the first four courses to form the base of the first pillar, using two full blocks as well as a third block split lengthwise in each course. This will make a solid, 800 mm-high base. Use two blocks per course for the rest of the pillar.

7 Build the wall sections in stretcher bond to a height of 8 courses, and the low planter wall to 2 courses. If 390 mm x 190 mm x 190 mm blocks are used, the wall will be about 200 mm thick once it has been rendered.
8 Use half blocks and broken blocks to build the capping on each pillar.
9 Once the mortar has set, render the surface, creating a lip on the top of the wall if you wish.
10 Ideally, keep the rendered surface damp for a few days before painting and planting.

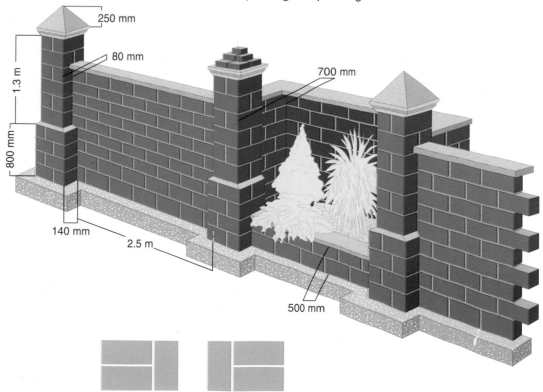

METRIC/IMPERIAL CONVERSION TABLE

To convert the measurements given in this book to imperial measurements, simply multiply the figure given in the text by the relevant number shown in the table alongside. Bear in mind that conversions will not necessarily work out exactly, and you will need to round the figure up or down slightly. (Do not use a combination of metric and imperial measurements – for accuracy, rather stick to one or the other system.)

TO CONVERT	MULTIPLY BY
millimetres to inches	0.0394
metres to feet	3.28
metres to yards	1.093
sq millimetres to sq inches	0.00155
sq metres to sq feet	10.76
sq metres to sq yards	1.195
cu metres to cu feet	35.31
cu metres to cu yards	1.308
grams to pounds	0.0022
kilograms to pounds	2.2046
litres to gallons	0.22